Issues in
Criminal Justice

edited by
Marc Riedel
Duncan Chappell

Published in cooperation with the
American Society of Criminology

The Praeger Special Studies program —
utilizing the most modern and efficient book
production techniques and a selective
worldwide distribution network — makes
available to the academic, government, and
business communities significant, timely
research in U.S. and international economic, social, and political development.

Issues in
Criminal Justice:
Planning and Evaluation

Praeger Publishers   New York   Washington   London

PRAEGER SPECIAL STUDIES IN U.S. ECONOMIC, SOCIAL, AND POLITICAL ISSUES

Library of Congress Cataloging in Publication Data
Main entry under title:

Issues in criminal justice.

   (Praeger special studies in U.S. economic, social, and
political issues)
   1. Criminal justice, Administration of—United States—
Addresses, essays, lectures.   I. Riedel, Marc.
II. Chappell, Duncan.
HV8138.I85   1976   364   75-37767
ISBN 0-275-56280-8

PRAEGER PUBLISHERS
111 Fourth Avenue, New York, N.Y. 10003, U.S.A.

Published in the United States of America in 1976
by Praeger Publishers, Inc.

Printed in the United States of America

PREFACE

In November 1973, the American Society of Criminology held its annual meeting in New York. At the meeting several hundred scholars, concerned primarily with crime, delinquency, deviant behavior, and corrections, gathered to present papers and exchange views.

The present volume is a selection of papers that were delivered at the New York meeting. One of a series of books arising from that meeting, it is published in response to a demand that the research information, data, ideas, and proposals heard in New York be made permanently available to professionals, students, government officials, and others engaged in the effort to understand the phenomenon of crime in modern society.

The editors would like to express their appreciation to Steven T. Sowder, graduate student, Center for Studies in Criminology and Criminal Law, University of Pennsylvania, for additional editorial assistance. We are also grateful to Esther Lafair and Patricia Coyne for the many and yeoman secretarial services involved in the preparation of this volume.

The officers of the American Society of Criminology at the time of the New York meeting were Dr. John C. Ball (Temple University), President; Dr. Edward Sagarin (City University of New York), President-Elect; Dr. William E. Amos (U.S. Board of Parole), Vice-President; Dr. Nicholas Kittrie (American University Law School), Vice-President; Dr. Sawyer Sylvester (Bates College), Secretary-Treasurer; Dr. C. Ray Jeffrey (Florida State University), Editor, Criminology: An Interdisciplinary Journal.

CONTENTS

LIST OF TABLES

LIST OF FIGURES

Issues in
Criminal Justice

ISSUES IN CRIMINAL JUSTICE PLANNING AND EVALUATION

Marc Riedel

The ever-present concern of policy-makers, administrators, and funding sources to have an objective and rational basis upon which to allocate important resources has led to an increased demand and support for evaluation and planning of criminal justice programs. In some cases, funding sources, such as the Law Enforcement Assistance Administration (LEAA), require evaluation as part of the funding; but, increasingly, evaluation and planning are seen as an integral part of program development, management, and policy-making.

It is inevitable that with the growing importance of planning and evaluation, scholars and practitioners should be engaged in assessing the usefulness of these endeavors; the present collection of papers represents that kind of effort. By way of overview, the papers have been arranged in three groups. The first focuses on the outcomes of evaluation research, methods of achieving a wider dissemination of findings, and types of research methodologies and strategies. This first group includes discussions of the issues confronting evaluation researchers in their involvement with the broader social and political environment.

The second group of papers is oriented toward planning problems. Although the distinction between planning and evaluation is not easy to maintain and is, to some extent, an arbitrary one, this group emphasizes how programs are developed and implemented and the factors that lead to their demise and termination.

The final two papers discuss the broad assumptions of both planning and evaluation. In the Luger and Lobenthal paper, it is asked whether current planning is taking into account rapid social and technological change. Reiman, drawing implications from an analysis of John Rawls's A Theory of Justice, raises questions about the assumptions of two prominent delinquency theories.

Evaluation

Evaluation of criminal justice programs is an important part of planning and a source of information, ideas, and policy for administrators. The task that has traditionally been assigned to evaluation research is that of determining the effectiveness of criminal justice programs. In order to determine what types of programs are effective, Adams, in the first part of his paper, evaluates the evaluations of evaluation research. Of the seven studies reviewed, he says, "Some are much more skeptical than others, but all see research with practical payoff as being a small percentage of the total."

The standard of comparison for evaluation research is not absolute, but relative; how does the outcome of evaluation research in corrections compare with similar endeavors in other fields? Comparisons suggest that evaluation in corrections is just as productive as that in medicine or industry, according to Adams. Of course, what is true for corrections is not necessarily true for other aspects of criminal justice. Insofar as the application of controlled experimental design is concerned, it is more frequently used in corrections than in law enforcement and court programs.

A number of issues are implied or discussed by Adams in his paper. Turning to one—the comparison of evaluation research with research and development projects and biomedical research—we grant, at least for purposes of discussion, that the outcomes of evaluation research in corrections are no worse than the outcomes in medicine or industry. We must remember, however, that medicine and industry keep complete records of past programs that have been attempted and know to some extent why they have failed or showed positive outcomes. Research and development units and biomedical researchers also know under what conditions programs will show positive outcomes and under what conditions such outcomes cannot be expected because of the setting in which the program is carried out. What is the analogue to this in corrections research?

While the National Institute of Mental Health (NIMH) and LEAA have established reference services to disseminate past findings, the summaries of these findings have been limited. While these reference sources are useful in providing a bibliography, a comprehensive review of the literature as a prelude to proposing a program for funding remains a major effort. Important as the effort may be, the relationship to obtaining funds ultimately is unclear. Whether a program is funded depends less on the demonstrated success of similar programs in the past and more on the political and social context in which it is proposed. The "innovativeness" of many programs frequently consists of generating a different title for an old idea or inventing an ingenious acronym. Be that as it may, the development of retrieval and information systems that can summarize relevant past programs quickly and concisely is an important step forward.

To make available the results of past programs, Block and Ross document the development of a system to permit a quick and concise summary of the results of delinquency prevention programs. While they focused on delinquency prevention, the same methodology could be developed for many different programs in criminal justice. The methodology involves training raters to code programmatic and administrative variables so that they can be computer-processed. The output is of two types; a description of the program itself and a standardized report that enables the program to be compared with similar programs.

Useful as concise summaries of programs are to planners and policy-makers, the system developed by Block and Ross permits comparisons and analyses of the relative success of programs in relation to different measures of success and various independent variables. For example, in their analysis of delinquency programs, they found a strong inverse relationship between the use of a statistical technique to measure success and program success. Of twenty cases using statistical techniques, eleven were judged successful and eight failures; of twenty cases using nonstatistical techniques, nineteen claimed success and one claimed failure. Furthermore, although the relationship was not strong, programs with experimental evaluation designs were somewhat less likely to be judged successful in comparison with programs using quasi-experimental or nonexperimental designs. Twelve percent of the nonexperimental designs and 14 percent of the quasi-experimental designs were successful, but only 4 percent of the programs with experimental designs claimed success.

The results of the analysis by Block and Ross, as well as some of the authors reviewed by Adams, provide support for an almost unquestioning faith in experimental design as the best available means of program evaluation. In an examination of federal evaluation policy, Ball comments on the entrenched notion of the intrinsic superiority of the quantitative, experimental evaluation mode. According to him, the authors of Federal Evaluation Policy maintain "that where the assumptions underlying the classical experimental designs are not met, it is not possible to perform adequate evaluations" (original emphasis). The latter suggests that assumptions underlying experimental design frequently become synonymous with the blind insistence on quantification and one type of methodology. Such thinking is akin to identifying physical science with test tubes and Bunsen burners.

In addition to documenting the strong beliefs about appropriate methodology held by administrators and funding sources, Ball explores the shortcomings of classical experimental design in terms of selecting appropriate and relevant dependent variables, control over the conditions of the experiment, and the development of suitable indicators. He discusses how such qualitative techniques as the interview, experience survey, and the analysis of documents and records provide alternatives to a mode of evaluation frequently viewed by criminal justice practitioners as too artificial and unrealistic.

Rutman suggests that evaluation can be made more useful if we distinguish between demonstration and exploration programs and recognize that there are different evaluative strategies for each. As an early stage of program development, exploration programs permit creative people to express their innovativeness in programs that in the past have included residential "community-based" programs, diversionary projects that attempt to keep people out of courts and correctional institutions, and programs that explore different therapeutic methods.

To illustrate appropriate research strategies for explorations, Rutman draws on a research design prepared for a training center for community corrections. Rigorous experimental design would be difficult to use in testing the effect of innovative programs like this one because frequently they are vaguely conceptualized, without a clear orientation, and because the goals are vague, unarticulated, or conflicting. Instead, Rutman monitored the actual training sessions and did immediate and three-month follow-up interviews with the participants in the pilot program. Such material was essential to the planning of a demonstration program in which impact can be measured.

Demonstration programs are projects testing an alternative in the hope that if it is successful, it will find its way into general use. Evaluation of demonstration projects focuses on testing, through rigorous scientific methods, the effectiveness of a program in achieving its stated goals. Drawing illustrative material from a group probation project, Rutman discusses how measures can be specified and experimental and control groups established. Because goals are clearly delineated, important variables are clearer, thus permitting rigorous evaluation.

As important as consideration of types of methodology and the dissemination of results are in evaluative research, a central and pressing source of problems is the social and political setting in which the program is conducted. While it would be easy to believe that the values of scientific inquiry would dominate in the process of evaluation, in many cases it is a matter of uneasy coexistence. Boudouris finds that the evaluator is "faced with the conflicting goals of objective, evaluative research, and the public image that the administrator hopes to preserve. If he chooses to write a report with regard only for the truth, he faces not having his grant renewed. If he tries to write a report to please the administrator, the interest groups and the funding agencies, he has prostituted himself."

Boudouris suggests ways to avoid some of the dilemmas of evaluation. Where bureaucrats are willing to change, evaluators can look
for tradeoffs and ways to compromise with administrators that would
not damage the evaluators' integrity. What is needed is a regulatory
body to which the researcher can present his results. The existing
state and regional councils could serve as such a regulatory body if
they could be "de-bureaucratized and de-politicized." As it stands,
these councils are made up of city or state agencies or political offices.

Krisberg and Takagi discuss the social and political context of
planning and evaluation in criminal justice in a slightly different way.
Instead of examining how evaluation research is used, or not used, by
administrators and funding sources, they ask whose values or interests
are being furthered by the creation and funding of criminal justice programs. It is not a matter of evaluators vs. administrators or planners
vs. administrators; it is a matter of providing a program that the
community has defined in terms of its needs.

Criminal justice programs should be designed and implemented
with the active involvement of community members; to do otherwise
can have catastrophic results for a community. In the course of an
evaluation of San Francisco's Chinatown Youth Services, Krisberg
and Takagi concluded that many delinquency control programs are
imposed on communities from outside, without any real concern for
community benefit; they are "simply pretensions of charity which
mask the dynamics of internal colonization." Such planning and evaluation can increase divisiveness and distrust to the point where, in the
Chinatown project, the center director was killed by gang members.

Much of the preceding discussion has focused on the many difficulties in the relationship between research and public policy. It is
encouraging to find one area of criminal justice policy where research
does seem to have a noticeably positive impact. Bedau's paper discusses how research on the death penalty was used in Furman v.
Georgia and how the Supreme Court decision has led to a new research
agenda.

In finding the exercise of standardless judge and jury discretion
in imposing the death penalty to be constitutionally impermissible, the
effect of social science research upon the Court's thinking was clearly
evident. While not evaluation research in a conventional sense, and
while several of the dissenting Justices objected to the paucity and
insufficiency of death penalty research, all of them agreed on its relevance to the legal issues. Chief Justice Warren Burger, in dissenting, stated: "Data of more recent vintage is essential." Of the
majority Justices, he stated, "They share a willingness to make sweeping factual assertions, unsupported by empirical data." It is difficult
to think of other instances of research being given as prominent a
consideration in the formulation of law and policy.

While the existing research on the death penalty was useful, albeit in a limited way, the decision in Furman v. Georgia defined some
new factual issues for which little or no research was available. If
Furman had declared standardless judge or jury discretion unconstitutional, then a legislative alternative would be statutes that completely
eliminated sentencing discretion by making the death penalty mandatory
for certain offenses. A second alternative would involve the legislation
of standards to guide judge or jury discretion. Such "mandatory" or
"guided discretion" statutes were thought to meet the Supreme Court's
objection of arbitrariness in sentencing. One phase of the proposed
research agenda would focus on the effects of mandatory or guided discretion statutes on other parts of the criminal justice process. For
example, if the death penalty is mandatory for first-degree murder,
is there an increase in commutations during the mandatory period in
comparison with the period when the death penalty was imposed in a
discretionary fashion? Under the general hypothesis that discretion
eliminated at one decision point affects the pattern of discretionary
decisions before and after sentencing, the number and types of charges
at arrest, indictments, and plea bargaining during the discretionary
and mandatory period become important for ascertaining whether arbitrariness in sentencing continues to exist.

Planning

Planning efforts in criminal justice, just as in any other area,
proceed on a set of assumptions about the behavior of members of
other interdependent organizations. Efforts of persons proposing a
new program to initiate and involve other organizations in a cooperative relationship suggest the awareness of planners of the interdepen-
dency.

In discussing the planning and development of the office of an
ombudsman for the Connecticut correctional system, Hollander documents how numerous relationships with other organizations and groups
had to be created and sustained before a program could be implemented.
While it is too early to determine how effective the ombudsman will
be as part of the inmate grievance machinery, planning for various
contingencies that may arise was thorough.

From the description of the program there are two characteristics that should contribute to the success of the program. First,
every effort was made to obtain the views and support of the inmates
very early in the development of the program. The fears of the planning group were that if inmates were not involved in the early stages
of development, support for the program would be limited; these fears
never materialized.

Second, probably the greatest difficulty with an ombudsman program in any organization is maintaining the autonomy of the office.
The Hartford Institute attempted to do this by selecting a man for the
position who would not be identified with correctional administration
or inmates; such a selection would enhance the credibility of the ombudsman to both groups. In addition, procedures were carefully
worked out to insure that the ombudsman would have ready access to
the needed records and the opportunity to talk to relevant people involved in the grievance. Such procedural efforts, specifying the rights
and power of the office, should go far to make the ombudsman a valuable mediator of conflicts in correctional systems.

Important as the cultivation and maintenance of relationships
with other organizations are to a treatment program, the nature of
these interdependencies changes as members change roles. Krisberg
discusses the demise of the Urban Leadership Training Program as
members of the pilot project graduated and expected to be integrated
into the community. Graduates of the program found that funds were
no longer available for their community services.

Krisberg describes the rewards of the training program to the
university that financed it, the community that supported it, and the
staff that worked for it. He concludes, "Institutions and organizations
which sponsor delinquency prevention and resocialization programs
receive substantial benefits from such enterprises which need not be
related to successful program outcomes for the delinquents who participate in them. Indeed, planners, supporters and staff members
accrue many more rewards during a training process and greater
costs at the conclusion of such efforts." The absence of follow-up,
Krisberg implies, indicates that interested organizations have reaped
all the benefits they could and are no longer interested.

It is regrettable, if not inevitable, that the success of the most
careful planning depends upon the consistency of support from political
officials whose tenure in office is determined by elections. Lieberman
traces the efforts of the Illinois Department of Corrections to decen-
tralize the penitentiary system for all but the repetitively violent offenders. During 1971 and 1972 the Department completed planning
and had allocated full funds for the establishment of four community
treatment centers throughout the state. The project came to a halt in
1973 with a change in administration within the office of the Governor
and the Director of the Department of Corrections.

Lieberman suggests that such political changes may indicate a
growing sentiment away from community-based corrections. The
American citizenry may be more concerned with humane treatment
within correctional mega-institutions than in the correctional objective
of reintegration and community involvement.

Planning and Evaluation for the Future

By necessity planners are future-oriented; however, their success frequently depends on the futures they have in mind. Correctional planners, if Luger and Lobenthal are correct, have not cushioned themselves against "future shock"; they are not prepared to deal with the consequences of rapid social change that is bound to influence corrections. They examine the effect on corrections of available technology devised to control the offender, such as electronic surveillance techniques and sensory implants. They also consider the effect of changes in community power structure and expanding inmate rights.

Ultimately, how planning and evaluation are carried out depends upon what we construe as the criminal or delinquent. It is appropriate that the final paper is directed toward examining the consequences for criminology of developments in the philosophy of justice. If it is through philosophy that we become aware of central assumptions that guide our behavior and theorizing, then emerging theories of justice may offer alternative ways of viewing crime, and the planning and evaluating of criminal justice. Reiman explores this problem by examining the implications for criminological theory of Rawls's A Theory of Justice.

2

EVALUATIVE RESEARCH
IN CORRECTIONS:
STATUS AND PROSPECTS

Stuart Adams

By many indications, criminal justice is facing an evaluation crisis. Billions of dollars are being earmarked for new criminal justice programs, and pressures for evaluation are rising. At the same time, complaints about ineffective measurement and wasted research resources also are rising. We are troubled by confusion over research methods and strategies, by shortages of good evaluators, and by indifference to research on the part of many administrators and officials.

This is clearly a time for taking stock. What is the present status of criminal justice evaluation? What kinds of evaluation, if any, are paying off? What will the evaluative research of tomorrow be like? And who will be doing it?

These issues have been addressed in a volume prepared for the National Institute of Law Enforcement and Criminal Justice, research arm of the Law Enforcement Assistance Administration. The work was done by the Advanced Institute for Studies in Crime and Justice, a research unit within the American University Law School. The volume, Evaluative Research in Corrections: A Practical Guide, outlines for administrators and researchers how assessment in corrections and criminal justice can be improved (Adams, 1975). The present paper summarizes some portions of the volume.

This article has also appeared in Federal Probation, March 1974. Evaluative Research was developed under contract with the National Institute of Law Enforcement and Criminal Justice. The opinions expressed here are the author's.

Evaluation Today

What is the present status of evaluation in corrections? One approach to this question is through currently available reviews of research. Vast numbers of evaluative studies have been done in corrections over the past fifteen or twenty years. Although there has been no systematic appraisal of this body of research, several fragmentary evaluations have been made.

W. C. Bailey reviewed and assessed 100 evaluative reports from the whole range of correctional studies and found them to be mostly unsystematic or nonexperimental. They were deficient in good behavioral theory and generally unable to demonstrate positive effects from treatment. The studies included twenty-two experimental designs, nine of which reported statistically significant improvement associated with treatment. Bailey's final conclusion was: "It seems quite clear that . . . evidence supporting the efficacy of correctional treatment is slight, inconsistent, and of questionable reliability" (1970:738).

Adams (1967) reviewed twenty-two experimental studies of the effectiveness of reduced probation and parole caseloads in California. Thirteen (59 percent) of these experiments showed either significant reduction in recidivism or a benefit-cost ratio higher than unity.

J. Robison and G. Smith examined several studies, primarily controlled experiments, bearing upon major decision points in California corrections. They found "no evidence to support any program's claim to superior rehabilitative efficacy" (1971:80).

G. Kassebaum et al, in a massive controlled experimental study of group counseling in a California prison, reported negative findings. In widely ranging comments on other studies, they observed that in recent years negative findings have appeared in growing numbers in correctional evaluation. They surmised that corrections might become cool toward outside researchers and secretive about research findings because of this "dearth of good tidings for both the treatment specialists and the program administrators" (1971:309).

R. M. Martinson reviewed 231 published and unpublished evaluative studies of correctional programs, focusing on research of more rigorous kinds. He reported "little evidence . . . that any prevailing mode of treatment has a decisive effect in reducing the recidivism of convicted offenders" (1971:309).

D. C. Speer (1972) examined twenty-one controlled experimental studies of psychotherapy in corrections and identified eleven that included follow-up data on community performance after treatment. Of the eleven studies, six (55 percent) indicated a reduction in subsequent arrests and time spent in jail. The most definitive finding was that out of eight studies of juvenile treatment, six showed significant improvement; of the three involving adults, none showed significant improvement.

F. Berkowitz (1973) reviewed thirty-eight evaluative studies that were generally representative of 400 LEAA-funded projects under the California Council of Criminal Justice. Specified within the thirty-eight projects were 154 measurable objectives. Of these, sixty (or about 40 percent) were judged to have been achieved. The reviewer also identified seventy-three methodological deficiencies in the thirty-eight projects. Goal attainment was highest and deficiency rate lowest in the five experimental projects among the thirty-eight studies.

The conclusions from these seven evaluations of evaluation can be grouped under three headings.

Subjective Conclusions from Vaguely Defined Samples. The gist of three of the reviews is that correctional programs are not effective; that the most rigorous evaluative studies show few, if any, results; and that correctional managers may become concerned enough about this poor showing to exclude university researchers from agencies and to withhold negative findings from the public. The reviews are skeptical and polemical in tone; they question the integrity of correctional administrators; and they clearly ignore some impressive evidence of program effectiveness.

Objective Conclusions from Balanced Samples. Two of the reviews imply that a scanning of the spectrum of evaluative research in corrections will disclose some good research and some effective programs. The statistically significant positive findings, which tend to come primarily from controlled experimental studies, are relatively few. In the experimental designs, which make up from one-eighth to one-fourth of the reviewed studies, about half "pay off," in the sense of significant, positive findings.

Objective Conclusions from Selected Samples. The remaining two reviews indicate that if one takes only controlled experimental designs in selected areas of corrections, at least half of the studies will show either statistically significant effects associated with treatment or benefit-cost ratios higher than unity.

There are, clearly, sharp differences among these three groups of observers. Yet there is one sense in which all seven appear to agree. Some are much more skeptical than others, but all see research with practical payoff as being a small percentage of the total.

Is this good or bad, relatively? What does experience show in other fields? A. Gerstenfeld (1970:1) observes that "studies indicate that more than 50 percent of all R & D projects fail." J. W. Blood (1967:16) narrows this estimate a bit: "An average of four out of five engineers and scientists work on projects that do not reach commercial success." And L. P. Lessing (1950:115) quotes a former president of Du Pont as estimating that not more than one in twenty of Du Pont's research projects eventually pays off.

If we turn from high-technology industry to medicine, some of
the assessments are equally restrained. K. White (1973:23), in an article on medical progress, states that during three decades of intensive
biomedical research, there has been no improvement in life expectancy
of adults, and no discovery of "effective means . . . for coping with the
stubborn complex of social illnesses that now predominate in the economically advanced countries."

These are rough comparisons. They suggest, nevertheless, that
evaluation in corrections is as productive, generally speaking, as
evaluation in industry or medicine. We distinguish here between corrections and criminal justice as a totality. Evaluation in law enforcement and the courts seems less far along than in corrections, at least
insofar as the application of controlled experimental designs is concerned.

Worthwhile Kinds of Evaluation

If we conclude that correctional research is doing about as well
as can be expected under the circumstances, yet we would like it to do
better, what can we suggest? One possibility is to find out what kinds
of research pay off—and consider expanding those kinds. But what pays
off?

This brings us to case studies. In the absence of a computer
printout of all studies that have "made a difference"—that is, have had
a visible impact on correctional practice—in the past two decades, we
will take examples from recall.

Probation in California was a survey of sixty county probation
departments in the state of California in 1956 (Adams and Burdman,
1957). It found probation operations to be generally substandard in
comparison with the guidelines set forth by the professional associations. The study recommended a probation subsidy by the state to
bring county operations up to an acceptable level. The California Assembly at first rejected the recommendation, but after a follow-up
survey and the development of a performance-based subsidy plan that
carried important benefits for both state and counties, the recommendation was enacted into law (Smith, 1965; 1973a). Since 1965 an esti-
mated 40,000 California offenders have remained in the community
after conviction rather than going into state institutions (Smith, 1973b).

The "Preston Impact Study" examined the effects of a state
training school program on older delinquents (Adams, 1959). It used
tape-recorded interviews with a panel of subjects during their stays
at Preston to trace attitude and information changes. The study concluded from the developmental evidence thus disclosed that Preston was
anti-rehabilitative. It recommended to the executive staff of the Cali-

fornia Youth Authority (CYA) that a controlled experimental test of
community versus institutional treatment be set up to check this conclusion. Executive staff agreed—a risky decision, perhaps, since it
opened up the possibility that their empire would be dissolved if community treatment proved substantially more effective. [1]

The CYA Community Treatment Project (Warren, 1970) provided
the experimental test called for in the "Preston Impact Study." During
1961-74, CYA used an interpersonal-maturity typology, differential
treatment, ward-staff matching on personality and behavioral characteristics, and a complicated experimental design to study the comparative outcomes of community and institutional treatment. This landmark
project, some minor flaws notwithstanding, has strongly influenced
thought and planning in juvenile corrections not only in California but
also nationwide and worldwide.

Project Crossroads, in the District of Columbia (1968-71), also
had an impact. It was designed to explore the possibility of diverting
young first offenders from adjudication by providing counseling, job-
finding, educational placement, and other services during a ninety-day
period after arrest and before trial. Successful participation led to
dropping of adjudication. The project demonstrated, by means of a
quasi-experimental design, that recidivism rates were reduced significantly and that job status and earnings were upgraded (Leiberg et al,
1971). Economically, the project showed benefit–cost ratios of about
2 to 1. The project has now become part of the operations of the D.C.
Superior Court. Along with the Manhattan Court Employment Project,
it has served as a model for numerous pretrial diversion projects in the
nation. It also has led to Congressional interest (S. 798, Quentin Bur-
dick, and H. 9007, Thomas Railsback) in providing a sound legislative
base for pretrial diversion programs.

Another evaluative study that made a difference was a time-series
analysis, Narcotic-Involved Offenders in the D.C. Department of Corrections (Adams et al, 1969). This study found that rates of intake of
drug-involved offenders were describing an incipient exponential curve.
Intake, in ordinary language, had begun an abrupt shift from a long,
gradual rise to a steep, upward climb. The study recommended quick
development of community-based treatment in place of prison for these
offenders; otherwise the D.C. prisons would soon be vastly overloaded.
The result, within six months, was two halfway houses for narcotic-
involved offenders. Within twelve months these were expanded into a
District-wide Narcotics Treatment Administration—now apparently
necessary for what looked like a full-blown heroin epidemic in the District's high-risk population. Within two years the program grew into
(proportionately) the largest methadone maintenance treatment program
in the nation.

From these five cases, what can we say—tentatively—about evaluation projects that pay off?

First, all kinds of research designs are represented. This suggests that operational payoff can come from anywhere within the
methods spectrum, as W. C. Bailey and F. Berkowitz have shown.
The five cases included surveys, a panel interview, a time series, a
quasi experiment, and a very elaborate controlled experiment in three
phases: perhaps the most difficult and at the same time the most infor-
mative experiment thus far seen in the social-behavior field. Para-
doxically, the heaviest impact came from the crudest of the five
studies—the field survey of county probation departments—and the recommendations that followed from it.

Second, the five cases show that we often can get high impact
from a small study. The study of narcotics offenders took only a man-
month of time and cost at most $2,000, but it led to the rather prompt
establishment of one of the major narcotic-addiction treatment programs in the nation.

Third, projects with impact have thus far been changing the system rather than the offender. There seems to have been little gain
from attempts to "change the offender." A possible exception is the
D.C. Narcotics Treatment Administration, which has led to a marked
reduction in heroin use in the District. The reduction is viewed as
largely the result of attitudinal and behavioral changes by program cli-
entele (DuPont and Greene, 1973). It also may be argued that Community Treatment Project (CTP) was effective in changing its clients.
There is a tendency to dismiss CTP with such comments as, "Well,
it does at least as well as the institutional program, and it costs less."
This evaluation fails to give credit for the marked change in performance of selected categories among the various I-level types. It is
probable, however, that the major impact of CTP is to induce communities to provide increasingly for the treatment of juvenile delinquents
at the local rather than the state level. And in this respect, CTP is
much less potent than the probation subsidy.

Fourth, the projects with impact seem to come out of situations
where researchers actively make recommendations and follow through
on planning. Rather than finishing their work with a final report, they
conclude with both a final report and a documented plan for either a
more rigorous follow-on study or an action program.

Fifth, the projects with impact tend quickly to set off a chain of
actions and decisions by planners, administrators, and officials in
other agencies or political entities. This may occur because the impact project or study implies system change, which involves a widen-
ing circle of actors. Why the major impacts have thus far been system
change rather than offender change is not clear. The explanation may
simply be that it is futile to "tinker with" or "fine tune" the present

correctional process in the hope of making significant changes in offenders. In such cases, the only real option open to the researcher,
the correctional administrator, and the public is to seek major, constructive changes in the correctional system.

What do these five cases tell us about increasing the rate of payoff in correctional evaluation? Conduct more surveys? Engage in
more exploratory or nonexperimental studies? We could make clearer
decisions about this if we had an opportunity to examine a broader
range and larger number of case studies. We also could profit from
some advance knowledge about how much change and how much sta-
bility we are facing in the next decades. If change in corrections is
going to accelerate, we will need freer and more imaginative studies;
more resourcefulness and less mechanical following of traditional research rules.

Provisionally, then, payoff can come from any methodological
direction, so we should not become enamored of elaborate statistical
techniques or of controlled experimental designs—no more than circumstances warrant. It seems important also to shape evaluative procedures and subject matters more closely to the information
requirements and the decision needs of the time. For the present, it
appears wise to focus more on changing the system than on changing
the offender, accepting that at a later time the reverse emphasis
might become more appropriate. We need, of course, to learn how to
change the offender, although resources should not be expended heed-
lessly in attempting this through "unworkable" structures or procedures. And here we note that Speer and CTP make a partial case for
the possibility of changing youthful offenders, even within the present
system. [2] Finally, we appear to need a new breed of researchers—
people who can formulate realistic but innovative program plans as
well as execute competent studies in various research designs.

Tomorrow's Evaluative Research

What will tomorrow's evaluative research in corrections be like?
We must be tentative, again; but it seems that evaluation will become
more varied, focus less on certainty and more on utility of knowledge,
answer questions more quickly, and come from researchers who are
more flexible or adaptable—individuals who are increasingly making a
career of correctional research.

Campbell (1973:224) talks about "trapped" and "experimental"
administrators. The former are emotionally committed to their programs and tend occasionally to shelve or bury negative research findings. The latter are more detached and pragmatic; they regard

programs as something to be retained if they work and to be replaced
if they don't. We obviously need more experimental administrators as
heads of agencies.

We also need experimental rather than trapped researchers:
persons who don't have to "go by the book," who are comfortable with
a quasi experiment when a controlled experiment can't be done, who
can effectively use nonexperimental studies to aid planning and decision-
making, and who have an interest in contemporary methods—from cost-
benefit analysis to simulation.

In recent years there have been ten or more demonstration
projects in adult pretrial diversion, all carried out as quasi experiments. This development comes at a time when there is increasing
discussion about the unsuitability of the true experiment for action research in contemporary social agencies. The pretrial diversion studies
are providing at least partial validation for the argument that research
is tending to increase in both flexibility and power to have an impact. [3]

Tomorrow's Evaluators

Who is going to do the evaluation? Part of the evaluation crisis
is lack of staff, particularly the right kind of staff. Most state departments of correction lack research units. Most state planning agencies
for criminal justice programs also lack evaluators, although they are
receiving increasing support and guidance from LEAA in developing or
finding evaluative capability. The new National Association of State
Criminal Justice Planning Agencies should eventually prove to be
another important source of guidance and support.

In their search for evaluative capability, the state agencies are
not sure which way to turn. They are leaning, understandably, toward
evaluation of programs by outsiders: university faculty, consulting
firms, and research institutes. "You can't evaluate your own boss"
was the slogan at a recent regional meeting of state planning agency
evaluators (Southeast Evaluation Symposium, 1973). "Evaluation research is one of the few ways of keeping the corrections business
honest," one university professor remarked, apparently implying that
this can best be done from the outside (Ward, 1973:206).

LEAA, A. Etzioni, and N. P. Roos have complicated this dia-
logue in a number of ways. LEAA reported at a meeting on evaluation
called by the U.S. General Accounting Office early in 1973 that extensive failure resulted when research monies were given "hands-off" to
a number of selected universities. "Although a variety of methods
was used to carefully select the universities, LEAA was (hard) pressed
to identify any results from the research" (GAO, 1973:9).

Etzioni had remarked earlier that university faculty members were not good prospects for applied research tasks. They tended to turn the tasks into basic research projects in line with their own academic interests. Etzioni (1972:B-3) noted Roos's description of such practice as "Robin Hooding."

Evaluation by consulting firms also has its drawbacks. Roos observes that while the academic researcher is perhaps somewhat unresponsive to the decision-maker's needs, the consulting firm is likely to be oversensitive to the decision-maker's wishes. "Instances have been observed where a consulting organization asked to evaluate a program provides its client with a whitewash which the evaluator assumes, or has been told, the client expects" (Roos, 1973:297).

Are there solutions to these obviously serious problems with outside evaluation? With respect to university-based research, M. E. Brooks sees a need to change the academic reward structure.

That structure is not geared to encourage faculty participation in the evaluation of agency action programs. Confronted with time limitations, the need to gather and analyze data on projects designed by others . . . and a paucity of opportunity for career-boosting publications, most academicians prefer to remain aloof (Brooks, 1973:14).

While acknowledging that the university reward structure needs changing, Brooks is not sanguine. "We've known for a long time that it needs changing." As for consulting firms, he is equally pessimistic, and he has no suggestions to offer.

These capsule comments should not obscure the fact that some university faculty and some consulting organizations have done commendable work in evaluation. However, they underscore two conclusions. First, these outside evaluators must somehow be induced to raise the quality and relevance of their work. Second, the correctional administrator who seeks outside evaluation should realize the problems he faces and be prepared to deal with them more knowledgeably.

What of the correctional agencies themselves? To what extent should they plan to carry the bulk of evaluative research? Or should they accept the dictum "You can't evaluate your own boss"?

One issue is capability. The record here is favorable to the agency research units. If we compare the final agency reports on the PICO Project (Adams, 1970), the Community Treatment Project (Palmer, 1971), and the Youth Center Research Project (Jesness et al, 1972) with final university staff reports such as Street Gangs and Street Workers (Klein, 1971), C-Unit: Search for Community in Prison (Studt et al, 1968), and Prison Treatment and Parole Survival (Kassebaum et al, 1971), it is clear that the correctional agency research shows better design, more objective reporting, and products of greater utility to the decision-maker. This would argue for expanding agency research efforts.

The fairness of the foregoing comparison is not immediately evident. One can question the representativeness of both the research and the researchers. However, the point most worthy of emphasis here is that in the past twenty years the best evaluations of correctional agency programs have been done by agency research staff.

There is a second crucial issue—recruitment. Can capable persons be attracted to and retained in correctional or criminal justice research in sufficient numbers to meet the rising need? The recent history of recruitment shows young researchers staying with an agency only a short time—many soon return to the campus as teachers, occasionally becoming writers of polemics on corrections. The latter is understandable, given the dehumanizing and irrational aspects of the correctional enterprise. Nevertheless, it tends to complicate the staffing problem.

How, then, can agency evaluation units develop and improve themselves? Clearly, some thought to methods of attracting and retaining productive researchers is required. There is another possibility. R. E. Emrich (1973) has suggested that effective research staffers can be developed in-house. He proposes an "apprenticeship model" of evaluation, in which existing administrative or operational staff will undertake assessment of projects, receiving guidance as needed from researcher-consultants. In time the apprentices may become masters.

This proposal brings to mind the fact that some of the notable early studies in California corrections, particularly the Special Intensive Parole Unit (SIPU) in 1953-64 and the Pilot Intensive Counseling Organization (PICO) in 1955-61, were begun by operations or treatment staff, with outside consultation. And in the Los Angeles County Probation Department, six probation officers proposed and carried out a controlled experimental study of the effects of group counseling on juvenile probationers—an experiment that yielded positive results in a brief but workmanlike effort (Adams, 1965).

Critical as the staffing problem may be, its final resolution is difficult to foresee. If an on-the-spot recommendation were required, the evidence apparently supports wider development of correctional agency research units. Three such units have compiled good records of evaluative research production and program planning and development over the past several years. Furthermore, they have disseminated their major findings to a broad audience, apparently with good effect. These units now stand as models for other agencies. Their ability to combine superior research productivity with effective planning and development within the same unit makes them stand out in comparison with other possible sources of evaluation and planning. Their powerful role in technology transfer adds further to their importance as models.

There remain other issues that bear significantly on the prospects of correctional and criminal justice evaluative research. These can only be alluded to here. One is the matter of agency administration: effective evaluation and planning require pragmatic, experimental stances by forward-looking, supportive administrators. There is need for adequate organizational and fiscal support for research. There is need to eliminate the excessive level of trial-and-error in present-day evaluation, and to reduce some of the duplication in projects and evaluative studies between states.

The list can be expanded further. There is need for better use of theory as a guide to evaluation, and a need for long-range as well as short-range strategies for evaluation. There is need to encourage the development of a sound research tradition in corrections, relatively independent of academic departments and consulting organizations. And, finally, there is need for the encouragement and support of meaningful careers within the areas of correctional and criminal justice research.

Summing Up

In summary, correctional evaluation has been an active and relatively productive enterprise for more than twenty years. Its accomplishments may be compared favorably with achievements not only in social action fields but also in more remote kinds of endeavor.

Many of the products of evaluative research have had a strong effect on corrections and criminal justice, as shown by the Probation Subsidy Program in California, the Narcotics Treatment Administration in the District of Columbia, and the pretrial diversion programs now being developed in many states. In corrections, the impact of evaluation has shown up primarily as system change; there appears to be less evidence of progress in furthering offender change, except possibly with juvenile offenders.

The impact of evaluation thus far has come primarily from "weak" research designs that produce information of low certainty levels. Controlled experimental studies, or other "strong" designs, with perhaps one or two exceptions, have exerted little influence. More recently, the quasi experiment and cost-benefit analysis have been teamed successfully in efforts that have brought strong support to pretrial diversion as a criminal justice procedure.

What form correctional evaluation will take in the future depends largely upon the rapidity of change and the spread of systems thinking in criminal justice. It also depends upon the extent to which rational long-range strategies of evaluation emerge. The likelihood is strong that some forms of traditional evaluation (such as controlled experimentation) will decline in importance and that contemporary methods (cost-benefit analysis, operations research, systems analysis, and simulation) will grow in importance.

Staffing an expanding criminal justice evaluation effort poses some severe problems. Widespread disappointment with university-based and consulting-firm research and the relative success of agency-based research where there has been good support suggests that more emphasis should be placed on the latter approach to evaluation. However, there is also need to rationalize and make more responsible the contributions of university faculty and consulting organizations.

Given the development of several additional agency research units with high capability and more concern for the recruitment or development of "experimental" administrators of agencies, the groundwork may be laid for the emergence of a strong correctional research tradition based within corrections itself. Such a tradition would aid greatly in defining productive research models, recruiting and retaining promising staff, making possible significant correctional research careers, and speeding the development of a more rational criminal justice process.

Notes

1. A form of dissolution is being proposed for the California Youth Authority by Senate Bill 391, which would merge the diminished CYA with the adult Department of Corrections.

2. Speer's discovery that 75 percent of the experiments with juvenile offenders in psychotherapy result in significant reductions in recidivism may, of course, have practical implications for only a small portion of the total juvenile offender population—those in need of and amenable to psychotherapy as now practiced.

3. Project Crossroads is a good illustration of resourcefulness in criminal justice research under difficult conditions.

References

Adams, S.
    1959   The Preston Impact Study. Sacramento: California Youth
            Authority. Unpublished report.
    1965   An experimental assessment of group counseling with juvenile
            probationers. Journal of the California Probation, Parole
            and Correctional Association 2 (Spring): 19-25.
    1967   Some findings from correctional caseload research. Federal
            Probation 31 (December): 48-57.
    1970   "The PICO project." Pp. 548-61 in N. Johnston, L. Savitz,
            and M. E. Wolfgang, eds., The Sociology of Punishment and
            Correction. 2nd ed. New York: Wiley.
    1975   Evaluative Research in Corrections: A Practical Guide.
            Washington, D.C.: U.S. Government Printing Office.
Adams, S., and M. Burdman
    1957   Probation in California. Sacramento: Special Study Com-
            mission on Correctional Facilities and Services.
Adams, S., C. Reynolds, and D. F. Meadows
    1969   Narcotic-Involved Offenders in the D.C. Department of Cor-
            rections. Research Report no. 12. Washington, D.C.: De-
            partment of Corrections.
Bailey, W. C.
    1970   Correctional outcome: an evaluation of 100 reports. Pp.
            733-42 in N. Johnston, L. Savitz, and M. E. Wolfgang, eds.,
            The Sociology of Punishment and Correction. 2nd ed. New
            York: Wiley.
Berkowitz, F.
    1973   Evaluation of Crime Control Programs in California: A Re-
            view. Sacramento: California Council on Criminal Justice.
Blood, J. W., ed.
    1967   Utilizing R & D By-Products. New York: American Manage-
            ment Association.
Brooks, M. E.
    1973   Dimensions of and constraints on evaluative research. Pro-
            ceedings. Southeast Evaluation Symposium. Raleigh: North
            Carolina State Planning Agency.
Campbell, D. T.
    1973   "Reforms as experiments." Pp. 187-225 in J. A. Caporaso
            and L. L. Roos, Jr., eds., Quasi-Experimental Approaches.
            Evanston, Ill.: Northwestern University Press.
DuPont, R. L., and M. H. Greene
    1973   The dynamics of a heroin addiction epidemic. Science 181
            (August 24): 716-22.

Emrich, R. E.
    1973   Models for the evaluation of state criminal justice programs.
            Proceedings: Research Workshop. San Francisco: California
            Probation, Parole and Correctional Association.
Etzioni, A.
    1972   Redirecting research dollars. P. B-3 in Washington Post,
            June 11.
General Accounting Office
    1973   Evaluation of Law Enforcement Assistance Administration
            Programs: A Conference Summary. Washington, D.C.: Na-
            tional Academy of Public Administration and U.S. General
            Accounting Office.
Gerstenfeld, A.
    1970   Effective Management of Research and Development. Read-
            ing, Mass.: Addison Wesley.
Jesness, C., et al.
    1972   The Youth Center Research Project. 2 vols. Sacramento:
            American Justice Institute.
Kassebaum, G., D. A. Ward, and D. M. Wilner
    1971   Prison Treatment and Parole Survival. New York: Wiley.
Klein, M. W.
    1971   Street Gangs and Street Workers. Englewood Cliffs, N.J.:
            Prentice-Hall.
Leiberg, L., R. Rovner-Pieczenik, and J. F. Holahan
    1971   Project Crossroads. 3 vols. Washington, D.C.: National
            Committe for Children and Youth.
Lessing, L. P.
    1950   The world of du Pont: how to win at research. Fortune 42
            (October): 115-34.
Martinson, R. M.
    1971   Treatment Evaluation Survey. Unpublished. Cited in Kasse-
            baum et al., supra, p. 309.
Palmer, T. B.
    1971   California's community treatment project for delinquents.
            Journal of Research in Crime and Delinquency 8 (January):
            74-82.
Robison, J., and G. Smith
    1971   The effectiveness of correctional programs. Crime and
            Delinquency 17 (January): 67-80.
Roos, N. P.
    1973   Evaluation, quasi-experimentation and public policy. Pp.
            281-304 in J. A. Caporaso and L. L. Roos, Jr., eds., supra.
Smith, R. L.
    1965   The Board of Corrections Probation Study. Sacramento:
            California Board of Corrections.

1973a The Quiet Revolution. (SRS) 73-26011. Washington, D.C.: Department of Health, Education and Welfare.
1973b Personal communication (taped interview).
Southeast Evaluation Symposium
1973 Proceedings. Raleigh: North Carolina State Planning Agency.
Speer, D. C.
1972 The role of the crisis intervention model in the rehabilitation of criminal offenders. Buffalo: Erie County Suicide Prevention and Crisis Service. Unpublished paper.
Studt, E., S. L. Messinger, and T. P. Wilson
1968 C-Unit: Search for Community in Prison. New York: Russell Sage.
Ward, D. A.
1973 Evaluative research for corrections. Pp. 184-206 in Lloyd E. Ohlin, ed., Prisoners in America. Englewood Cliffs, N.J.: Prentice-Hall.
Warren, M. Q.
1970 The community treatment project. Pp. 671-83 in Norman Johnston et al., eds., Sociology of Punishment and Correction. New York: Wiley.
White, K.
1973 Life and death and medicine. Scientific American 229 (September): 22-33.

A TECHNIQUE FOR UTILIZING PRECODED VARIABLES IN THE REVIEW OF PROGRAMS IN CRIMINAL JUSTICE RESEARCH

Richard Block and David J. Ross

In the field of criminal justice research, and especially in the study of delinquency, there is a recognized need to make available the results of earlier programs to those designing new programs for crime prevention.[1] Thus NIMH and LEAA have established reference services to disseminate the findings of past research. A major problem with these abstracting services has been a lack of summarization. The planner must read through nonsystematized reviews of dozens of programs and try to abstract relevant findings himself, if these findings are included at all.

There have been at least three major reviews of delinquency-prevention literature. Two of these considered correlates of program success, primarily the use of statistical or nonstatistical analysis; however, these analysis reviews consider only a limited number of variables and are of little use in describing a particular program. Thus, one form of review supplies a good description of past research and findings through abstraction without a summarization of these findings (LEAA), while in another form analytic reviews are limited to only a few variables and allow no description of particular programs (Logan).

This paper documents the development of a system of detailed program abstracting that will permit quick and concise summarization and analysis. In this paper only one form of program, that for delinquency prevention, will be discussed; but the same methodology could be developed for analyzing and describing many different programs in the criminal justice system.

Precoded Review: A Pilot Program

The pilot program of analysis and summarization reported here grew out of an attempt to define delinquency in order to develop methods to analyze the success or failure of particular delinquency-prevention programs. In order to develop a definition of delinquency with some relevance for delinquency-prevention programs, many programs were reviewed and their success at preventing delinquency was recorded. While this review was being compiled, it became clear that its usefulness would be improved by summarization and that there were certain similarities between programs that would allow for the application of computer techniques and standard social science analysis to summarize these programs. It also was clear that if a detailed description of the nature and success of a delinquency-prevention program could be translated into code for computer analysis, this code could be retranslated into standardized English for easy reading and comparison by laymen not experienced in computer techniques. Additionally, the retranslation could be used in a cataloged procedure that would make available reviews of programs with only certain characteristics. A code book was therefore developed for the computerized summary of delinquency-prevention programs. The summaries were intended to be self-contained, with full documentation of sources as well as computerized descriptions of the programs.

What variables should be included in this code book? It was apparent that the first variable was whether the program succeeded in reducing delinquency. In addition, what other measures of program success could be assessed, and how was success in these measures analyzed? Finally, what independent variables might be useful in describing programs and analyzing the bases of the programs' success? Five sets of independent variables were developed: administration, type of juveniles included in the program, causes of delinquency, type of treatment, and design of the evaluation research.

Administrative variables included both the personnel of the program and the physical and fiscal nature of the problem: variables used included employment of new personnel, type of structure housing the program, administration of the program, and source of funds. Among the variables concerned with type of juvenile were length of time in programs, the measures used to select juveniles, and a modification of the Warren (1972) scale of offender typologies. "Causes of delinquency" included most theories of delinquency in current usage. If a program stated no explicit cause of delinquency, this also was noted. Ten different methods of treatment were included as variables for analysis. This list proved inadequate, primarily because of a failure to differentiate forms of counseling treatment but also because of the innovativeness of program directors. A variable was created to count the number of treatments used. This list will be revised in the future reviews.

Among the variables used to describe the evaluation technique of a program, the most complex was a coding for approximation to a classic experimental design; other variables included the number of cases in the experimental and control groups, the nature of assignment to these groups, and the use of statistical analysis. The full code book and marginals for this pilot program are available from the Urban Institute.

The four most serious problems that developed in this pilot program were the lack of immediate access to complete records of each program; the inability to code most variables for all programs; the difficulty in training coders who could achieve a high degree of reliability; and the use of reviews that depended upon the potentially biased reports of program evaluators.

Few programs fully reported their methodology or the nature of the sampling technique used. Some reported planned designs rather than the program as it developed. A related but independent problem was that the design of any one program might include less than half the variables that potentially could be coded. Thus, many programs were not concerned with causes of delinquency, and many reports of delinquency-prevention programs did not measure success in reducing delinquency. The lack of relationship between the review coding and the actual operation of programs limited the number of cases for some analyses.

The coders used in this review had to have both knowledge of criminological theory and social science research in order to develop a common set of definitions. In the pilot program this was not easy to achieve. The full-scale development of this program would use, at least initially, two coders for each program. Results would be checked for intercoder reliability, precedents would have to be set for disagreements.

Finally, the project is a review of evaluations that for the most part were performed by professionals hired by the project they were evaluating. This means that the evaluators may not have been unbiased and may have inadvertently emphasized success aspects. Thus, this review of evaluations is ultimately dependent on the evaluation of the original investigator.

A Program Review

Once coding is completed, the data are available for both review and analysis. As a system of review, this would be very useful to program planners. A planner could call for reviews of all programs based upon a particular theory of delinquency, using a particular form of therapy, or that have been successful in reducing delinquency or promoting attitude change. Figure 3.1 is an example of the review program, since the coded data are rendered into reasonably intelligible English. In a future form of this program, a noncoded but computerized description of each program, similar to that of the NIMH literature review, will be included. Thus, the planner will have two intelligible program reviews, one in a form standardized for all programs and another in a form particular to the program itself. A reprint of the program used to translate code into English is available on request.

Many planners would not be satisfied merely knowing what programs had been formulated, but might ask for a summary and analysis of programs. What questions, therefore, can be answered using this computerized review? Among the types of questions that could be analyzed are the following:

1. What theories of delinquency most typically underlie delinquency-prevention programs? Of the seventy-eight programs analyzed, 30 percent mentioned family relationships as a cause of delinquency, compared with one program that mentioned no explicit theory.
2. What forms of treatment are most frequently used in preventing delinquency? In this pilot analysis of seventy-eight programs, the most frequently used techniques concentrated on altering individual behavior. Thus, 76 percent of the programs used some form of counseling therapy, and 55 percent used educational therapy. Ten percent of the programs used some diversionary technique, and 23 percent used some form of community or halfway house.

Most planners would not be content with these relatively simple summaries, but might find cross-tabular analysis or summaries of cross-tabular analysis very useful in their planning. Thus, questions of the relative success of different types of programs, or the relationship between length of time in a program and the success of a program, might be important considerations.

Success in delinquency-prevention programs may be measured in several ways. First, by the evaluator's statement, did it reduce delinquency? But there are other possible measures of success. In the following analysis three measures of success are used: reduction in delinquency, reduction in recidivism, and positive attitude change. These were the three most commonly mentioned measures of success in the pilot program.

FIGURE 3.1

A Precoded Treatment Review Translated into English

RAYMOND J.ADAMEK AND EDWARD Z.DAGER
AMERICAN SOCIOLOGICAL REVIEW 33 6 D68 P931-44
SOCIAL STRUCTURE IDENTIFICATION AND CHANGE IN A TREATMENT-ORIENTED INSTITUTION

ID NUMBER IS 32
HIGHEST POSITION OF RESEARCHER IS PHD
YEAR OF PUBLICATION OF REPORT 1968
YEAR PROGRAM BEGAN 1966
YEAR PROGRAM COMPLETED 1966
ARTICLE FROM ASR PUBLICATION
LOCATION OF STUDY OTHER REFORMATORY
TYPE OF LOCATION URBAN SMSA
MAJOR SOURCE OF FUNDS PRIVATE FOUNDATION
MINOR SOURCE OF FUNDS NO OTHER
WHO EMPLOYS RESEARCHER? UNIVERSITY OR RESEARCH ORGANIZATION
AGENCY ADMINISTERING PROGRAM PRIVATE FOUNDATION
TYPE OF EXPERIMENTAL DESIGN USED EXPERIMENTAL-T2
LENGTH OF TIME SUBJECT IN THE PROGRAM 3-6 MONTHS
TYPE OF STUDY CASE STUDY
CRITERIA EMPLOYED FOR ADMISSION NOT CLEARLY STATED
SEX OF SAMPLE FEMALE
RACE OF SAMPLE NOT USED AS CRITERION
EDUCATION CRITERION FOR ADMISSION SPECIFIC EDUCATIONAL LEVEL
VIOLENCE CRITERION FOR ADMISSION SPECIFICALLY NONVIOLENT
COMMUNITY CRITERION FOR ADMISSION NOT USED AS CRITERION
PSYCHOLOGICAL CRITERION USED MINOR OR NO PSYCHOLOGICAL PROBLEMS
SOCIOLOGICAL CRITERION USED NOT USED AS CRITERION
AGE OF THE SUBJECT TEEN-AGER
RECORD OF THE SUBJECT NO OTHER
OTHER CRITERIA FOR SUBJECT INCLUSION NO OTHER
COULD SUBJECT BE REMOVED FROM PROGRAM? UNCLEAR
NUMBER OF CASES IN EXPERIMENTAL GROUP 119
NUMBER OF CASES IN CONTROL GROUP ZERO
TYPE OF CONTROL USED NOT USED AS CRITERION
FAMILY POSTULATED AS CAUSE OF DELINQUENCY NOT USED AS CRITERION
COMMUNITY POSTULATED AS CAUSE OF DELINQUENCY NOT USED AS CRITERION
PEER GROUP POSTULATED AS CAUSE OF DELINQUENCY YES
SCHOOL POSTULATED AS CAUSE OF DELINQUENCY NOT USED AS CRITERION
CULTURE POSTULATED AS CAUSE OF DELINQUENCY NOT USED AS CRITERION
POLICE POSTULATED AS CAUSE OF DELINQUENCY NOT USED AS CRITERION
PHYSIOLOGICAL CAUSE FOR DELINQUENCY NOT USED AS CRITERION
PSYCHOLOGICAL CAUSE FOR DELINQUENCY NOT USED AS CRITERION
REFERENCE GROUP CAUSE OF DELINQUENCY YES
LABELING PROCESS CAUSE OF DELINQUENCY NOT USED AS CRITERION
CHARACTERISTICS OF SUBJECTS IN PROGRAM WERE CONFORMIST AND NOT USED AS CRITERIA
GROUP AND INDIVIDUAL COUNSELING USED YES
EDUCATION USED NO
PSYCHOTHERAPY USED NO
PAROLE OR PROBATION USED NO
TRADITIONAL PRISON PROGRAMS USED YES
SOCIAL WORK, COMMUNITY SERVICE, RECREATION USED NO
WORK THERAPY OR TRAINING YES
EXCLUSION FROM LABELING NO
GROUP HOMES, HALFWAY HOUSES NO
MISCELLANEOUS PROGRAMS USED YES
RECIDIVISM AS CRITERION FOR SUCCESS NOT USED AS CRITERION
REDUCTION IN DELINQUENCY NOT USED AS CRITERION
COMMUNITY CHANGE NOT USED AS CRITERION
EDUCATIONAL ACHIEVEMENT NOT USED AS CRITERION
COST REDUCTION NOT USED AS CRITERION
PEER GROUP CHANGE NOT USED AS CRITERION
DIVERSION TECHNIQUES NOT USED AS CRITERION
ATTITUDE CHANGE GOOD SUCCESS-STATISTICAL
OTHER SUCCESS CRITERIA NO
RESPONSE BY COMMUNITY NOT USED AS CRITERION
RESPONSE BY ADMINISTRATOR COOPERATIVE
SUBJECTS RESPONSE TO PROGRAM COOPERATIVE
RESPONSE BY GUARDS OR STAFF COOPERATIVE
ALTERATIONS DURING PROGRAM NOT USED AS CRITERIA
WHO ADMINISTERED THE PROGRAM SAME INSTITUTION'S STAFF AND OTHER JUVENILES

The following analysis considers the relationship between program success and treatment used. Table 3.1 shows the relationship between type of treatment and the different measures of success.

The relative success of two types of programs stands out in this analysis. First, programs that utilized halfway houses, community live-in centers, or some other variation on the community home were more likely to be judged successful by their evaluators on all three measures than programs not using this technique. Second, programs that utilized traditional types of social work techniques were not as likely as others to be judged successful on any of the three measures.

The relative success of other programs is dependent upon what is being measured. For example, counseling had no effect on reducing either delinquency or recidivism but had a positive affect on attitude change. Educational programs were as successful as programs that did not use education in reducing recidivism, but they were substantially less successful in reducing delinquency or promoting attitude change.

A similar analysis was carried out to test the relative success of programs using a particular theory in comparison with programs that did not use that theory. As is clear from Table 3.2, the results were fairly dismaying. No theory had a strong positive relationship with program success, and the use of several theories was related to program failure.

It occurred to the designers of this program review that programs with no explicit theory of delinquency might be more successful than programs with an explicit theory. This, of course, did not mean that these programs lacked a theoretical base but, rather, that they were less concerned with theory than with development of treatment techniques. As seen in the last column of Table 3.2, this was the case. Programs that stated no explicit theory were more likely to be judged successful by their evaluators than were programs with explicit theories. Of seventeen programs with no explicit theory that measured reduction of delinquency, five (29 percent) were judged highly successful in reducing delinquency. Of twenty-six programs with explicit theories, two were judged highly successful in reducing delinquency (8 percent).

It was thought that the greater success of programs with no explicit theory might be explained by their concurrent lack of good experimental design or statistical measurement. This, however, was not found to be the case. Programs without explicit theories tend to use better experimental designs and are more likely to use statistical measurements of success than are programs with explicit theories.

That social work programs are not often successful or that programs without explicit theories are judged more successful by their evaluators than programs that did have them is valuable information

TABLE 3.1

Gamma, Method Used, and Success in Delinquency Prevention as Measured by
Recidivism, Reduction in Delinquency, and Attitude Change
(by treatment)

Success Measure	Treatment Used						
	Counseling	Education	Psychiatry	Parole	Social Work	Job Training	Halfway Houses
Recidivism	.00	+.01	-.22	+.71	-.35	+.38	+.34
Reduction in Delinquency	.00	-.34	-.03	+.08	-.32	+.15	+.16
Attitude Change	+.26	-.53	+.17	+.12	-.21	-.05	+.25

Note: A positive gamma indicates that programs that used a particular technique were more frequently judged as successful by their evaluators than programs that did not use that technique. A negative gamma has the opposite meaning.

Source: Compiled by the author.

TABLE 3.2

Gamma, Theory Used, and Success in Delinquency Prevention as Measured by
Recidivism, Reduction in Delinquency, and Attitude Change
(by theory)

Success Measure	Theory Used								
	Family	Community	Peer	School	Culture	Psychological	Reference Group	Labeling	No Explicit Theory
Recidivism	-.37	-.39	-.50	-.36	-.39	+.06	-.11	+.19	+.27
Reduction in Delinquency	-.58	-.52	-.43	-.24	-.50	-.17	-.42	+.11	+.38
Attitude Change	-.17	-.11	-.37	-.50	+.03	-.06	-.29	+.27	+.18

Source: Compiled by the author.

for policy planners. However, these conclusions cannot be properly
reached from the data of this pilot program. First, the number of
cases investigated is far too small—for example, only seventeen programs reviewed used parole services. Second, the analysis fails to
take into account systematic variation in evaluation techniques for different types of programs that might lead the evaluators of a particular
type of program to judge the program to be more successful than other
programs that achieve objectively similar results. Third, particular
types of programs or programs with particular theories might be more
able to limit their clients than other programs. Halfway house programs typically are limited to juveniles who would be acceptable in the
community. The next section of this paper considers possible methods
for dealing with the second problem, biased evaluation techniques.

Evaluation Design and Program Success

A systematic evaluation of a group of programs with a similar
goal can be very useful for policy-planning analysis. This review contains two sets of variables that would be particularly useful for this
purpose. Administrative variables included sources of funds, administrative control, location, duration, and year of program, and types
of employees; the second set of variables was concerned with the nature of the program evaluation, degree of conformity to the classic
experimental designs, the nature of the control group (if any), number
of cases in the experimental and control groups, and use of statistical
analysis.

In their analyses of crime-prevention programs, both Bailey
(1971) and Logan (1972) found a strong negative relationship between
the use of statistics and program success. This finding was confirmed
in the pilot program. As shown in Table 3.3, of twenty-three cases
that measured success in reducing delinquency using some statistical
technique, eleven were judged as highly successful or successful and
eight were judged as failures. Of twenty cases using nonstatistical
measures of success in reducing delinquency, nineteen claimed high
success or success and none admitted failure. Table 3.3 also shows
that similar relationships occur between the use of statistical techniques of evaluation and success in reducing recidivism and creating
positive attitude change.

Tables 3.4-3.6 demonstrate the relationship between the research design of a particular program and the success of the program
as stated by its evaluator. If it is assumed that the more closely a
program approximates a classic experimental design, the more valid
its evaluation, then a program with an experimental and a control

32   ISSUES IN CRIMINAL JUSTICE

group measured before and after an experiment would have a more valid research design than a program that only measured an experimental
group after the experiment occurred.

Program evaluations are divided into three types: those with experimental and control groups measured before and after the experiment, those in which there are at least two measurements (quasi
experiments), and those in which only the experimental group was
measured, and that group only once (nonexperimental) (Campbell and
Stanley, 1963).

The first thing to be noted in Tables 3.4-3.6 is the surprisingly
high percentage of programs that did not measure success in reducing
recidivism or delinquency, or changing the attitudes of their clients.
Fifty-seven percent of all experimental designs did not measure reduction in recidivism.

Programs with experimental evaluation designs were somewhat
less likely to be judged successful by their evaluator when compared
with programs having quasi-experimental designs or nonexperimental
designs. For example, 4 percent of the experimental programs that
evaluated reduction in delinquency were judged to be highly successful,
as compared with 14 percent of the quasi-experimental and 12 percent
of the nonexperimental designs. Overall this relationship is not very
strong.

TABLE 3.3

Percentage Distribution of Measures of Success by
Use of Statistical Measurements
(in percentages)

	High Success	Medium Success	Low Success	Failure	N (cases)
Recidivism					
Statistical	27	35	8	31	26
Nonstatistical	27	60	13	0	15
Reduction in De-					
linquency Acts					
Statistical	22	26	17	35	23
Nonstatistical	10	85	5	0	20
Attitude Change					
Statistical	11	68	11	11	19
Nonstatistical	15	67	11	7	27

Source: Compiled by the author.

TABLE 3.4

Percentage Distribution of Program Design by Reduction in Recidivism

Reduction in Recidivism	Design		
	Experimental	Quasi-Experimental	Not Experimental
Not mentioned	57	38	46
High success	7	17	18
Medium success	25	28	18
Low success	4	7	6
Failure	7	10	12
N	28	29	17

Source: Compiled by the author.

TABLE 3.5

Percentage Distribution of Program Design by Reduction in Delinquent Acts

Reduction in Delinquent Acts	Design		
	Experimental	Quasi-Experimental	Not Experimental
Not mentioned	50	41	41
High success	4	14	12
Medium success	25	31	35
Low success	11	3	6
Failure	11	10	6
N	28	29	17

Source: Compiled by the author.

TABLE 3.6

Percentage Distribution of Program Design by Attitude Change

Change in Attitude	Design		
	Experimental	Quasi-Experimental	Not Experimental
Not mentioned	46	38	35
High success	—	17	6
Medium success	39	38	47
Low success	7	7	6
Failure	7	—	6
N	28	29	17

Source: Compiled by the author.

Summary and Discussion

In this paper a new method for review and analysis of programs
in the criminal justice system has been proposed and demonstrated in
a pilot project review of seventy-eight delinquency-prevention programs. Utilizing computer technology, this review system is based
upon a set of precoded variables that are applicable to many programs
in delinquency prevention. These precoded variables can be analyzed
by means of standard techniques of behavioral science or can be retranslated into English for the use of program planners.

In the code book developed for delinquency-prevention programs,
six sets of variables were developed: administration, type of juveniles
included, causes of delinquency, type of treatment, evaluation design,
and program success by several definitions. After discussing problems that developed in this pilot program, several examples are given
of the use of this review technique for analysis.

The primary advantage of this form of systematic review over
other review systems developed in the criminal justice system is its
threefold utility. First, a standard review of the literature in a field
is created that is easily interpreted by laymen not trained in computer
sciences; second, a cataloging procedure is created that allows for a
systematic review of programs with only certain characteristics; third,
data are available for program analysis by policy and program planners
and behavioral scientists using standard analytic techniques.

Note

1. See Harlow (1969); Logan (1972:378); Bailey (1971).

References

Bailey, Walter C.
    1971   An evaluation of 100 studies of correctional outcome. Pp.
            733-42 in Norman Johnston et al., eds., The Sociology of
            Punishment and Correction. New York: Wiley.
Campbell, D. T., and J. Stanley
    1963   Experimental and Quasi-Experimental Designs for Research.
            Chicago: Rand-McNally.
Harlow, Eleanor
    1969   Prevention of Crime and Delinquency. New York: National
            Council on Crime and Delinquency Center for Programs.

Logan, Charles H.
    1972   Evaluation research in crime and delinquency: a reappraisal.
             Journal of Criminal Law, Criminology, and Police Science
             63, no. 3:378.
Warren, M. Q.
    1972   Classification of offenders as an aid to efficient manage-
             ment and effective treatment. Journal of Criminal Law,
             Criminology, and Police Science 62 (March): 239-58.

4

QUALITATIVE EVALUATION
OF CRIMINAL JUSTICE
PROGRAMS

Richard A. Ball

The suddenly increased emphasis on evaluation of criminal justice programs in recent years presents both significant opportunities and potential dangers. The opportunities are obvious; it may be possible to systematically increase the effectiveness of programs and to arrive at a much sounder basis for allocation of scarce social resources. The dangers lie in the American predilection for rushing into a conceptual wilderness with the axes of "know-how" and in our impatience with counsels of caution and pleas for a moment of reconnoitering. Yet it is an axiom of logic that the solution to a problem tends to hinge primarily on a proper statement of the issue. One who is concerned with improved evaluation has two principal recourses. First, it is possible to discover in the literature realistic accounts of success and failure, criticism and explicit commentary derived from such firsthand experience, and suggestions for exploration of alternative designs and modes of implementation. One might then gather those who have been deeply involved in attempts to design and conduct evaluation at various levels of responsibility and problem complexity, and draw upon their combined experience. The purpose here is to develop certain premises that have evolved from such an exploration and to argue for increased use of qualitative methodology in the evaluation of criminal justice policies, programs, and projects.

The opportunity to explore these issues with those deeply engaged in evaluating the criminal justice system resulted from a four-day conference of evaluators, of which the author was a director, during the summer of 1973. This conference, funded by the Law Enforcement Assistance Administration (LEAA), included representatives from

Reprinted by permission of the publisher, from Criminal Justice Research, edited by Emilio Viano (Lexington, Mass.: Lexington Books, D. C. Heath and Company, 1975).

each of the criminal justice state planning agencies in LEAA Region IV
(Delaware, District of Columbia, Maryland, Pennsylvania, Virginia,
and West Virginia), an interested evaluator from the Connecticut State
Planning Agency, a number of recognized authorities on the evaluation
of social action programs, and representatives from the Region IV
headquarters and the National Institute of Law Enforcement and Criminal Justice (NILECJ). In preparation for the conference, extensive
attention was devoted to the various critiques of available conceptuali-
zations and methodological approaches to the evaluation of social action
programs. A preliminary list of issues was developed on the basis of
this review, solicitation of issues from those scheduled to attend, and
the experiences of the author himself ranging from curriculum evaluation for the Department of Defense and evaluation of university programs through evaluation of correctional officers' training projects
and OEO-sponsored community action programs. As had been anticipated, the inadequacies of contemporary evaluation theory became a
major focus of the conference and a great deal of time was devoted to
the exposure of operating premises and the consideration of alternatives. Since, however, such interaction typically opens many basic
issues without resolving them, the discussions have provoked further
reflection and have led to this attempt at synthesis.

Dominance of Experimental Design

Any argument for the merits of qualitative approaches to the
evaluation of social action programs must face the resistance of the
more orthodox point of view. This position is put very clearly by J.
Wholey et al. (1970:87) in Federal Evaluation Policy.

> The principles of modern experimental design provide
> the basis for estimating the amounts and directions of
> program effects. Experimental design allows us to test
> hypotheses about program effects so that extraneous fac-
> tors can be excluded or corrected for, clearing the way
> for reasonable inferences about those factors in which we
> are interested. If the extraneous factors are no longer
> a threat to adequate inference, we are then in a position
> to rule out—among the set of "plausible" hypotheses—
> those which are not sustained by the results given by the
> study.

In contrast with the apparently rigorous quantitative research
design that tends to arbitrarily define certain elements as interchange-
able so that numbers may be assigned and manipulated according to
impressively elaborate formulas, qualitative designs may seem at the
very least fuzzy-minded. Thus, perhaps the first step in their advocacy

must be a clarification of the limits of quantitative, experimental or "quasi-experimental" models. In recent years some have begun to take a second look at the use of these deceptively reassuring models in social research generally (Phillips, 1971), while others have questioned in particular their applicability to the evaluation of social action programs (Weiss and Rein, 1970).

The experimental models are, of course, generally built upon premises that are very demanding. Hypotheses must be made clear, specific, and empirically testable through available research technique; and, to be of more than ad hoc interest, they must be derived from a systematic body of theory. These same premises demand control of relevant variables that might influence the outcome of the "experiment" through such techniques as matching or random assignment, and tend to rest upon assumptions that cause-effect relationships underline events. The experimental design has proved to be a tool of awesome power. Respect for these techniques actually implies, however, that we will be selective in our use and that the designs will be employed only under circumstances in which the critical premises hold.

Some indication of the prevalence of circumstances suitable for quantitative, experimental or "quasi-experimental" evaluation may be gained from an examination of Table 4.1, which shows clearly the problems faced in terms of existing quantitative methodologies. The notion of the intrinsic superiority of the quantitative, experimental evaluation mode is so entrenched, however, that Wholey et al. conclude their critique by maintaining that where the assumptions underlying the classical experimental designs are not met, it is not possible to perform adequate evaluations. Examination of the table tends to lead to depressing conclusions, especially since the problems involved in the evaluation of criminal justice programs are as serious as any encountered in public policy evaluation to date. When the problem of criminal justice evaluation is defined as a question of how to apply some type of experimental design to the study of public policy consequences, the problems may appear to be insoluble. However, it may be that the present impasse can be traced to an incorrect definition of the problem. Rather than reject the possibility of sound evaluation, one might better search for alternative methods, approaches suitable to the complex nature of social reality.

Fortunately, the limitations of experimental design have gradually become more obvious. Without the aura of "hard science" that surrounds these techniques, they would be questioned even more vigorously. Certainly the questioning would be facilitated by a knowledge of alternative possibilities, and it is to these—the so-called qualitative methods—that evaluators must turn some attention. Our own experience indicates that little knowledge of these methods, and less aware-

TABLE 4.1

Preliminary Estimates on Existence of Conditions for Evaluation
of Selected Federal Programs

Program	Agency	Availability of Suitable Output Measures	Availability of Measures of Appropriate Environmental Variables	Availability of Appropriate Comparison Groups	Availability of Measures of Appropriate Input and Process Variables
Manpower development and training programs	DOL	+	0	0	+
Neighborhood Youth Corps (NYC)	DOL/OEO	+	0	0	+
Work Incentive Program (WIN)	DOL/HEW	+	0	0	+
Vocational education	HEW	+	0	-	0
Follow Through	HEW	+	+	+	0
Job Corps	OEO/DOL	0	0	0	+
Head Start	OEO/HEW	+	+	-	0
Legal services program	OEO	0	0	+	0
Community action program	OEO	0	0	-	0
Urban renewal	HUD	0	0	0	0
Model Cities	HUD	0	0	0	0

Code: +: Existing methodology is sufficient and readily available for immediate application to evaluation.

0: Methodology is not advanced, and application cannot be made with complete confidence. Development of methodology will be a critical part of the evaluation.

-: Methodology unavailable. Development of an applicable method appeared unlikely at this time.

Source: Adapted from Wholey et al. (1970:109).

ness of their potential reliability and validity, exists among evaluators
of criminal justice programs. Similar implications may be drawn from
the work of those concerned with providing guidelines for criminal justice evaluators (Maltz, 1972).

The Potential of Qualitative Designs

One social research technique that is as powerful as it is overlooked is the simple interview. It can range in time from a few minutes
(perhaps seconds) to hours. Format can vary from a fixed forced-
choice schedule to informal conversation. One especially valuable var-
iant is the "focused interview" (Merton and Kendall, 1946). Frequency
may be limited to one interview, or the interviewer may return. It
may be desirable to interview a given respondent in several different
ways over time. Data so obtained may be subjected to reliability estimates on an inter-interviewer, inter-respondent, or inter-technique
basis or combinations of all of these. Of course, data reliability and
validity are vital considerations here, just as they are elsewhere. In
fact, it is largely the concern for validity that has led to this argument
for a return to face-to-face contact with data itself.
          The conversation is also of special value when handled so that the
investigator can talk with various individuals again and again as the research unfolds. In this way he can pursue a point dropped earlier because it became too touchy or because more promising topics arose
at the time. He can "forget" something said before and open the subject to check the consistency of his informant. He can return to an
issue, having learned more about it in the interim. He can choose the
best occasions for certain discussions without being forced to attempt
them at a less opportune time.
          When tied to the judicious use of interviews and conversations,
the "experience survey" (Selltiz et al., 1962:55) is another valuable
means of acquiring data. Many people are in a position to closely observe the process with which the investigator is concerned, and this
experience can be assembled and synthesized. The experience survey
proceeds by a purposive sampling that selects informants from various levels and sectors in order to provide coverage of as many perspectives as possible. The sample of issues should be representative
of various levels of importance; different institutional areas; a range
from the open, public debates to closed, restricted decisions; long-
term and short-term issues; and problems resolved compared with
those still unresolved. As the investigator becomes more familiar
with the milieu, he will be able to add selected sampling dimensions
dependent upon factors that appear as more critical in the context. As

he learns more about the networks under investigation, it will be possible to augment the discussion of issues raised by the respondent
through consideration of concrete cases introduced by the interviewer.

Another very useful adjunct to the techniques described is the use
of documents and records. These provide a means of developing inves-
tigative leads, serve to fill in data gaps, and can be used to cross-
check information obtained in other ways. Several cautions should be
observed, since it is possible that the researcher has been given access to a biased sample of materials. It is important to obtain whatever "clearances" are necessary to permit the study of as wide a
sample as possible. One must also be alert for means of detecting the
extent to which records have been altered (in extreme cases) or tem-
porarily removed. Unfortunately, many researchers have little training in the use of such materials. Most need assistance in determing
what they are seeking, how to recognize it when discovered, and how
to evaluate the reliability of various sources. Obviously, an "insider"
is a critical asset at this point. Despite the difficulties and the often
tedious nature of the "digging," ingenious use of these sources can
make a major difference in the quality of the final product.

The techniques of anthropological research, especially as combined with ethnomethodology (Denzin, 1969) and such tested tools for
the study of political processess as "events analyses" (Dahl, 1961), can
open many doors. As is implied in much of the foregoing, the various
research techniques should be supported by participant observation.
S. T. Bruyn (1966) has provided an excellent discussion of the rationale and uses of this approach. Ideally, participant observation allows
the investigator to share in activities as a normal part of the life under
observation. As B. H. Junker (1960:35-38) points out in his monograph
on fieldwork, the nature of this role may vary from the "complete participant" ("insider") through the "participant as observer" (in which
participation is primary) to the "observer as participant" (in which
observation is primary) and the "complete observer" ("outsider") who
watches from a social distance even if physically close to the action.
Above all, the observer must be in a receptive frame of mind, avoiding the imposition of a priori categories on the data.

Issues of Criteria Selection

Painful experience seems to have led those who have been wres-
tling with the day-to-day problems of evaluating the criminal justice
system toward a healthy skepticism regarding orthodox techniques.
Judging from the conference discribed above, there is a developing
sense that experimental design is too often "unrealistic." It would

seem that the practitioners agree with the conclusions of those academic critics who maintain that the model is too artificial to impose upon the typical situation and that it provides much too limited an account of events. There is, for example, the problem of the criteria for selection of criteria. That is, in what terms is the evaluation to be conducted? What are the program goals, and how is success to be measured? The evaluator who attempts the development of operational definitions suitable for quantification tends to stumble over one of the major myths of American society—the myth of value consensus. The truth of the matter seems to be that, while the "public" vigorously affirms such notions as "freedom," "democracy," and "crime reduction" in the abstract, individuals and interest groups often disagree violently with respect to who is to be granted what degree of "freedom," as to how much "democracy" is to be tolerated under what conditions, and as to what sorts of "crimes" should be reduced and which methods are acceptable for the accomplishment of any such end. Insensitive to this sociocultural diversity, the evaluator has tended to accept the particular version of reality held by his patron, to reify this conception of things, and to proceed somewhat uncritically with the application of measures conveying an appearance of scientific precision. Put in terms of measurement theory, validity has been sacrificed to reliability. As Howard Becker (1967) has pointed out, social scientists have tended to operate upon the basis of an implicit "hierarchy of credibility," in which the definitions of events supplied by the more powerful or prestigious are given greater weight in determining the reality of the situation. But there is a growing awareness among evaluators who have become sensitive to the social control dimensions implicit in all programs of social action. Thus, criminal justice evaluators now voice interest in the possible "political implications" of programs aimed at crime control and express some concern over their own role as possible legitimators of what may, from some perspectives, be viewed as repression.

If evaluation is to proceed realistically, qualitatively differentiated and conflicting goals must be recognized and incorporated in the design rather than being oversimplified or ignored altogether. The very nature of the "crime problem" itself may be posed differently by those of different class origins or political convictions, and one interest group may judge some given means of "crime reduction" as "successful" while another may term it a "failure". Calculations based upon these conflicting criteria may supply helpful data and should be undertaken if possible. Following the literature, we may conclude that one group seeks "efficiency" (calculable in terms of cost per service output unit delivered), another seeks "effectiveness" (a ratio of "success" to "failure" units), another seeks "adequacy" (ratio of "success" units to potential "problem" units available), and yet another seeks "preventive impact" (a reduction in problem units requiring service). But the problem remains that data alone cannot determine who is correct. It is in this sense that the "crime problem" is a political problem that must be solved politically rather than an "objective" phenomenon that can be resolved from a purely technical viewpoint. Although a careful diagnosis can clarify the nature of the problem, the decision for or against social surgery must be left to the patients, who will weigh risks in terms of their own values.

Perhaps the most important virtue of the qualitative methodologies lies in the fact that they are built upon a recognition of the complex nature of social reality. If we agree that situations are defined and that social reality is "constructed" (Berger and Luckmann, 1966) out of these different definitions, then it is easy to see that the evaluator faces not a simple world of "facts" but, rather, a congeries of overlapping social realities. One reason for the skeptical attitude of many experienced politicians and administrators toward the attempts at evaluation of social action programs is their realization that the artificial world of the usual quantitative or experimental design provides a caricature of the realities with which they must deal. It is not surprising that they will voluntarily use the design only when it seems clear that the results will support policy preferences reached more "realistically." Only when evaluative research becomes politically and socially realistic through a consideration of the "real world" will a contribution to that world be likely.

Issues of Experimental Controls

Another set of problems that has given rise to a search for alternatives to the traditional experimental design springs from the disillusionment experienced by every evaluator upon the discovery that he has very little control over the conditions of the "experiment." Although E. A. Suchman (1967) indicates that it is necessary to the method to assume that "the particular time at which the evaluation is made is 'typical' and that the program itself is highly stable and will not undergo constant revision," such circumstances are rare indeed. To complicate matters further, "the crucial question for the present analysis of evaluative designs in public service research is to what extent may the effectiveness of public service programs be due to faith or the symbolic power of official agencies rather than the intrinsic components of the system?" (Suchman, 1967:97). The usual quantitative or experimental design actually tends to obscure this fundamental question.

Fortunately, qualitative methods offer a means to deal with these harsh facts of life. One is encouraged to produce "working hypotheses"

that can guide him through uncharted and shifting events in lieu of a
rigid quantitative-experimental model that will very likely become
something of an obstacle between himself and the data. Flexibility is
the name of the game here. The evaluator becomes more opportunist
and less ritualist. He follows unexpected leads rather than preordained
maps. Of course, risk is concomitant with opportunity. The orthodox
role of technician is attractive partly because one can maintain his
"objectivity" as a defense against criticism or personal attack; but when
"objectivity" becomes a means of avoiding available data, the critics
who label program evaluation as mere "lip service" are close to the
mark.

Measurement Problems

        Still another set of problems has to do with the development of
indicators that can be rigorously specified and measured. As Robert
Weiss and Martin Rein (1970) have pointed out, the simple cause-effect
model has less relevance in a complicated, interdependent, and changing social milieu. In the latter case, any singling out of "independent"
and "dependent" variables is largely a matter of which segment of a
continuous chain of events is selected for study. The search for
"causes" of crime has taught us that "causes" are often "effects" seen
from a different perspective. This in turn implies that the allegedly
neutral evaluator may be identifying with the limited perspective of
one group over another in the selection of variables. Furthermore, he
usually will be forced to measure the critical variables selected (such
as criminal behavior) by some proxy variable (such as crime rates)
that is of questionable validity and is subject to manipulation by those
concerned that the evaluation produce certain outcomes. All in all, use
of the experimental model under such circumstances amounts to a re-
striction of science to fit the values, interests, and definition of reality
held by limited segments of society. Since the problem has been defined in terms acceptable to these particular segments and since the
experimental model provides little possibility for exploration beyond
preestablished formal channels of data analysis, there is minimal
chance that the conventional viewpoint will be endangered. If the continued existence of the problem is the price to be paid for preservation
of the conventional definitions of social reality, then the odds are heavily in favor of this outcome.
        The qualitative approach, on the other hand, concentrates on an
opening of alternative definitions, on the systemic conception of variables imbedded in a dialectic relationship rather than a cause-effect
sequence, and on the deliberate use of various types of measures de-

signed to illuminate the same underlying dimension. Given the exigencies of time and resources, the qualitative approach will opt for development of several gross measures that tap different aspects of a complex and highly abstract variable. Faced with the same strictures, the quantitative approach will tend to select one operational measure and direct time and resources toward increased precision within a highly limited framework. The qualitative approach is preoccupied with validity; the quantitative is preoccupied with reliability. But it must be emphasized that if validity is made primary, as ought to be the case, then one will also make sounder use of quantitative technique. It is possible through "triangulation" (Webb, 1970), for example, to develop a number of highly reliable measures of a given variable and to regard each as providing a valid indication of some aspect of the qualitative whole from a particular perspective. In this way greater validity is achieved through a combination of measures, with no sacrifice of reliability. And to regard the data as qualitative will not rule out statistical manipulation. In recent years there has been much progress in techniques, allowing even the application of multivariate analysis to qualitative data. It must be emphasized that the introduction of qualitative techniques must be complementary. Quantification is not to be repudiated but, rather, is to be used whenever appropriate.

Qualitative techniques can also contribute a great deal toward the development of theory. The fact that some have despaired of the possibilities here may be traced in part to the dominance of the orthodox models. Such designs may allow assessment of success or failure in some arbitrary terms; but they provide little indication as to "why," except for the questionable assumption that results may be attributed to the "independent variables." Qualitative methods, on the other hand, are ideally suited to an intensive consideration of the process by which effects are produced, particularly the possible influence of uncontrolled factors.

Research also has demonstrated the potential of qualitative methodology for the discovery of "unanticipated consequences" that tend to be overlooked by strictly quantitative techniques simply because the formulas are somewhat insensitive to factors not foreseen and incorporated at the onset of research. At this stage of the development of evaluative research, every means possible should be employed to disclose the unexpected and to probe its dimensions. Rather than assume the "closed system" model upon which the variations of experimental design rest, our methods must recognize that social programs are "open systems" constantly bombarded by external forces.

Conclusion

Following E. A. Suchman (1967:61) one may categorize criteria according to which the success or failure of a program may be evaluated in terms of effort (input assessment), effectiveness (output assessment), impact (output relative to need), cost effectiveness (input/impact ratio), and process (descriptive and diagnostic analysis of process by which results are produced). The use of qualitative methods will prove valuable no matter which criterion is employed, but the real power of the approach lies in its potential for the study of process. Unfortunately, it is just this set of issues that is most often ignored. Suchman (1967:66) takes the orthodox position and proceeds to suggest that the study of process "is not an inherent part of evaluative research." Here is the issue exactly. The study of process is crucial. Qualitative techniques are able to provide the needed contextual descriptions that quasi-experimental designs tend to assume as constants. The evaluator is in a better position to observe the particular forms taken in various contexts by programs often assumed to be completely standardized. Furthermore, one may be able to explain why certain variants tend to manifest themselves under given circumstances and to provide data of value in the redesigning of programs.

To the extent that conventional definitions are regarded as exhaustive of reality, variations of experimental design may seem ideal. If, on the other hand, validity is granted to conflicting definitions, the qualitative approach may be appealing. And it is the same with role image as with problem definition. That is, the experimental or quasi-experimental design will tend to appeal to the evaluator who regards himself as a technician devoted to rendering certain essentially valid a priori conceptions of reality more precise and reliable, while qualitative approaches will tend to appeal to the evaluator who sees himself as a social clinician (Gouldner, 1965) with the task of clarifying and unraveling contradictory assumptions, values, and interests that confuse social issues and impede possible solutions. To the latter, the study of process may appear to be a neglected gateway to evaluation of criminal justice programs, with increased use of qualitative methodology as one of the promising keys.

References

Becker, H.
    1967   Whose side are we on? Social Problems 14 (Winter): 239-48.

Berger, P. L., and T. Luckmann
    1966   Social Construction of Reality. Garden City, N. Y.: Double-
            day.
Bruyn, S. T.
    1966   The Human Perspective in Sociology. Englewood Cliffs,
            N. J.: Prentice-Hall.
Dahl, R. A.
    1961   Who Governs? New Haven, Conn.: Yale University Press.
Denzin, N. K.
    1969   Symbolic interactionism and ethnomethodology. American
            Sociological Review 34 (December): 922-33.
Gouldner, A. W.
    1965   Explorations in applied social science. Pp. 5-22 in Alvin
            W. Gouldner and S. M. Miller, eds., Applied Sociology.
            New York: Free Press.
Junker, B. H.
    1960   Field Work: An Introduction to the Social Sciences. Chicago:
            University of Chicago Press.
Maltz, M.
    1972   Evaluation of Crime Control Programs. Washington, D.C.:
            National Institute of Law Enforcement and Criminal Justice.
Merton, R. K., and P. L. Kendall
    1946   The focused interview. American Journal of Sociology 60
            (May): 541-57.
Phillips, D.
    1971   Knowledge from What? Chicago: Rand McNally.
Selltiz, C., M. Jahoda, M. Deutsch, and S. W. Cook
    1962   Research Methods in Social Relations. New York: Holt,
            Rinehart and Winston.
Suchman, E. A.
    1967   Evaluative Research. New York: Russell Sage Foundation.
Webb, E. J.
    1970   Unconventionality, triangulation and inference. Pp. 449-77
            in Norman K. Denzin, ed., The Research Act. Chicago:
            Aldine.
Weiss, R. S., and M. Rein
    1970   The evaluation of broad-aim programs: experimental design,
            its difficulties, and an alternative. Administrative Science
            Quarterly (March): 97-113.
Wholey, J., J. W. Scanlon, H. G. Duffy, J. S. Fukumoto, and L. M.
    Vogt
    1970   Federal Evaluation Policy. Washington, D.C.: Urban In-
            stitute.

5

EVALUATING EXPLORATIONS
AND DEMONSTRATIONS
FOR PLANNING IN
CRIMINAL JUSTICE

Leonard Rutman

In the past several years there has been an accelerating demand for the formal evaluation of human service programs. This interest is most dramatically reflected in the amount of funds, especially from the federal government, that have been allocated for the evaluation of sponsored programs. For example, G. N. Buchanan and J. S. Wholey (1972) noted that in three federal departments—Health, Education and Welfare, Housing and Urban Development, and Labor—there was a 30 percent increase in the amount of evaluation research funds allocated between fiscal years 1971 and 1973. Much of the impetus for evaluative research came from the program managers' concern to enhance program efficiency. Also, because of the relative scarcity of funds available for human service programs, funding bodies have increasingly demanded that objective data pertaining to program effectiveness be collected. This is a significant departure from the traditional reliance on testimonials provided by program personnel or selected clients. Additionally, the increased demand for the evaluation of human services has been spurred by the appearance of numerous research reports, across a variety of programs, that fail to demonstrate marked positive effects for the clients being served (Bailey, 1966; Eysenck, 1961; Fischer, 1973).

The increased emphasis on evaluation research is not totally a response to such external pressures. Human service professionals have become more interested and involved in conducting evaluative research for the purpose of testing theory and, ultimately, improving practice. Similarly, evaluation research is becoming increasingly accepted as an integral part of program development, program management, and policy-making. It is in this context that the demonstration

This article has also appeared in Journal of Sociology and Social Welfare (Summer 1975): 460-68. Published at University of Connecticut, West Hartford.

project has emerged as a popular planning strategy. In the field of
corrections the Ford Foundation and the President's Committee sponsored juvenile delinquency projects during the 1960s. More recently,
the Law Enforcement Assistance Act provides for the funding of "innovative" projects.

For planning purposes, it is generally expected that the lessons
learned from demonstrations, through the rigors of scientific research,
will result in large-scale adoption and major shifts in aims, styles,
resources, and effectiveness of human service programs. Although
the expressed purpose is to use demonstrations for social planning,
there are other covert purposes for undertaking such projects—
postponing needed action, placating particular constituencies, or chal-
lenging existing programs without a major concern for supporting data.
Under the rubric of demonstration projects are activities aimed primarily at the conceptualization and development of programs as well
as activities designed to test their effectiveness. A project aimed at
program conceptualization and development should be referred to as an
"exploration," and the term "demonstration" more appropriately re-
served for programs in which the independent variable (the program)
is clearly defined and amenable to manipulation.

Such a distinction has not generally been drawn, however. Thus,
in reference to the delinquency and poverty projects of the 1960s, Peter
Marris and Martin Rein state: "Though they claimed to be experiments,
their whole manner of operation seems more consistent with an exploration" (1969:207). Failure to make this distinction can result in poorly
conceived and inappropriately conducted evaluative research and, consequently, a limitation on the use of explorations and demonstrations
as instruments for social planning. The distinction between explorations and demonstrations will be emphasized in this paper in order to
show the differences in the purposes and evaluative research strategies
for both types of projects. Since the strategies of explorations and demonstrations represent stages of program development, the contribution
that investigations of these projects make to the planning process constitutes the overall context for examining evaluative research. Illustrative material will be drawn from two research designs prepared by
the author: an exploratory project, "The Training Center for Community Corrections," and a demonstration, "The Group Probation Project."

Evaluating Explorations: The Training Center

Alice Rivlin (1971) aptly described the strategy for program development in the 1960s as "random innovation" in which new ideas,
methods, and models were not systematized through experimental

methods. Her observation was not made disparagingly, for she recognized that such a climate permits creative people to develop innovative
programs. Examples of random innovations in the field of corrections
are plentiful: the trend toward various residential "community-based"
programs; diversionary projects that aim at keeping persons out of the
courts and correctional institutions; the use of ex-offenders in treatment programs; and the reliance of different therapeutic methods, including restitution as a rehabilitative approach. Although random
innovation results in the implementation of new ideas and methods, at
some point systematic experimentation is needed to determine the effectiveness of these programs. This involves the use of scientific experiments, to the extent possible, to test programs in different places
and under varying conditions.

　　Although information about the effectiveness of innovative projects may be desired, a host of factors besides the usually articulated
ones of political, legal, and ethical constraints impede the use of experimental methods to study these programs. Among numerous other
circumstances, the use of rigorous experimental designs in testing the
effects of innovative programs is greatly restricted by the characteristics of the program itself: vaguely conceptualized and operationalized
programs without a clear orientation and/or vague, unarticulated, and
conflicting goals. Martin Trow (1971) suggests that in such situations,
it is important that the research be in the service of the innovative
enterprise and not sitting in judgment of it. Research can contribute to
innovative projects and their ultimate use for program planning by as-
sisting program personnel in developing an impact model—including
the identification and operationalization of goals, the description of the
input or program variables, and an elaboration of a rationale that speci-
fies the relationship between the input variables and the stated goals
(Freeman and Sherwood, 1971). Exploration can be a useful strategy
for developing such an impact model, which could then be tested ex-
perimentally during a subsequent demonstration stage.

　　The research design used for the Training Center for Community
Corrections in Minnesota, an LEAA-funded project, will illustrate the
use of an exploration for developing a testable demonstration. The
Center was funded on the premise that since there was a dramatic increase in the number of community-based programs in Minnesota,
there must be a need for training personnel who worked in this field:

> The rapid emergence of new ideas and new priorities in
> the field of corrections has created a serious need for new
> training methods to develop the skills and knowledge nec-
> essary to translate the new correctional thinking and rhet-
> oric into action and to stimulate substantive reform in the
> correctional process.

Nevertheless, because of the newness of the field, there was no well-documented body of data that would clearly describe all the specific skills and knowledge necessary to implement community-based programs for which training was needed. The tasks facing the Center were developing an appropriate training program and identifying the goals that such training presumably would accomplish. The completion of this task would make it possible to measure the effectiveness of the training provided in the subsequent stages of the Center's development—that is, during the demonstration stage.

The initial task of the planning process was the determination of training needs. Staff representatives from sixteen operating residential programs in the pilot training group were invited to a needs/resource analysis seminar. The seminar was designed to help the participants identify areas of concern, translate those concerns into performance objectives, determine the kind of training that could best accomplish the stated objectives, and indentify the available training resources among the representatives and their programs. This seminar, however, was only a first step toward the identification of training needs. Two additional strategies were developed—a program follow-up and personal training inventory. Two staff members from the Center met with the entire staff of each of the pilot programs to discuss the outcome of the needs/resource analysis seminar. This meeting also focused on the particular concerns and training requirements of each individual program. To gather information on the perceived training needs of the personnel, each director and staff person was asked to complete a personal training inventory form. In addition, information was collected to identify resource persons whose knowledge and skills could be shared with others, either in formal sessions or on a consulting basis.

On the basis of the data collected from the needs/resource analysis seminar, the program follow-up, and the personal training inventory, the Training Center staff identified topics for pilot training sessions. Several one-day training sessions were planned and conducted. For research purposes, these sessions would provide opportunities for learning about preferred content, teaching approaches, instructors, and other concerns related to the provision of training for workers in community corrections. It was hoped that from the lessons learned in conducting these exploratory sessions, it would be possible to develop a testable training package. These sessions would also assist the Training Center in identifying goals that become apparent only through involvement in the training endeavor.

The research strategies for examining these pilot training sessions included monitoring the actual training sessions, immediate follow-up interviews with participants, and a subsequent three-month follow-up. Training Center staff who monitored each of the training sessions kept notes on the content covered, the teaching approaches

used, and the perceived reactions of the participants to the sessions.
The aim was to learn, through observation, the participants' training
needs and the preferred methods of instruction. To supplement the im-
pressions of the staff who monitored the training sessions, telephone
interviews were conducted with the participants within days of the actual training. These interviews yielded data on the participants' reaction to the training sessions and solicited their preferences for future
training. These data were useful in the ongoing process of planning a
demonstration project for training personnel in community corrections.
In regard to specifying goals, the staff could have determined the goals
for the Training Center's program. However, to broaden the range of
possible goals for consideration, information was solicited from the
participants in the pilot training sessions regarding how they felt the
sessions affected their work, ways in which they continued to pursue
content covered at the sessions, and how they viewed themselves using
the Training Center on the basis of their involvement in its activities.
As a result of this inquiry, unanticipated goals emerged. Finally, a
rationale could be developed for linking a planned training program to
specified objectives (for instance, persons participating in training
sessions are more likely to use evaluative research procedures in their
work and are more highly rated as effective practitioners).

Evaluating Demonstrations: The Group Probation Project

Whereas the major purpose for doing research on explorations
was to collect information for use in developing an impact model, the
evaluation of a demonstration project aims to "test," through rigorous
scientific methods, the effectiveness of a program in achieving its
stated goals. There are two types of demonstration projects. Model
demonstrations involve the evaluation of programs under ideal circumstances, with a controlled experiment being preferred. What are usually considered as demonstrations, however, are prototypes in which
programs are tested in natural settings that presumably resemble the
conditions under which such programs might be introduced if they
prove successful. The model demonstration serves the purpose of
testing the validity of a particular approach as a means toward the
achievement of some desired objective, while the prototype demonstration tests the ability to institute a workable program in the "real world"
based on that approach (Suchman, 1971).
The Group Probation Project is a prototype demonstration that
aimed to test and compare the effectiveness of group work and casework services with juveniles on probation. An impact model was an
inherent feature of the grant application. The experimental input or

independent variable was group work service. More specifically, initially two different group work approaches would be tested—positive peer culture and the mediating approach. The experimental variable could be clearly conceptualized and operationalized. For example, the use of positive peer culture could be recognized by the following traits: frequent meetings (at least three or four per week), focus of the meetings mainly on one idividual, small number of group members (five to seven), rigid seating arrangements, extensive use of confrontation. This method was clearly different from the mediating approach, which focuses on the group as a whole and in which mutual support and aid are the characteristic interaction patterns. Moreover, both group work approaches constituted a treatment distinctly different from the regular casework supervision. The outcome goals also were clearly stated: improved self-concept, improved school grades and attendance, reduction in delinquent behavior. The rationale linking the experimental input to the stated goals was that the peer group is more likely to have a positive influence on the youth's behavior than is the intervention by the professional probation officer.

The preconditions did exist for developing an experimental design; and compromises in this ideal design would be necessitated by professional, administrative, and legal constraints, but not primarily because of the limitations imposed by the characteristics of the program. The fact that juveniles are assigned to workers according to their geographical location posed limitations on the extent to which random assignment to experimental (group work) and control groups (casework supervision) could be made. Where random assignment was not possible, a comparative caseload was selected. "Before" measures of self-concept, school performance, family closeness, prior involvement with the court, and other relevant data could be obtained before placement on probation. Information could be collected on the treatment process (such as the use of contact sheets, completed by the workers, to measure the number and type of contacts made with the juvenile or on his behalf; group summary forms, completed by the worker after each group meeting, to note the focus of the meeting and the nature of participation by the members; videotape, to rate the workers' performance in the groups; and a questionnaire soliciting information from the juveniles about their views of the group). Finally, follow-up information could be collected on the juveniles in both the experimental and control groups after six months on probation.

This experimental design could address itself the following purposes for an evaluative study: effort—who received the service, who provided the service, how the program was implemented, the nature of the clients' participation, their view of the service received, resources needed to carry out such a program; effect—inferring the extent to which the program produced changes in school performance,

delinquent acts committed, and self-concept; and efficiency—comparative cost of providing group work and casework service relative to the
success of these two approaches. In other words, such an evaluative
study pursued two major goals: identifying the manner in which the
program was carried out, particularly determining whether it was actually implemented in the intended manner; and assessing and accounting for the impact of the program on the consumers of the service,
including the economy of the program in relation to accomplished results.

Comparative Analysis

Explorations and demonstrations have been presented as both
strategies and stages of a rational planning process. To maximize
their "payoff" for the planning enterprise, emphasis has been placed
on the use of evaluative research designs and procedures that are appropriate to the purpose and stage of the program's development. The
danger of emphasizing the differences in the purposes and research
strategies for explorations and demonstrations is the possibility of
creating artificial distinctions while negating important similarities.
Although a comparative analysis focuses on differences, the activities
of describing process, measuring outcomes, and inferring causal explanations are aims of all projects. Nevertheless, there is a difference
in the relative importance and nature of these activities according to
the type of project.

The research conducted on explorations is clearly aimed at discovery and relies largely on an inductive approach. In undertaking an
exploration, the pilot project affords a learning opportunity, with research used as a tool for collecting data to assist in the conceptualization and operationalization of a program and the specification of its
goals. This necessitates an emphasis on studying the program's un-
folding process:

> The whole process—the false starts, frustrations, adap-
> tations, the successive recasting of intentions, the detours
> and conflicts—need to be comprehended. Only then can we
> understand what has been achieved and learn from experi-
> ence (Marris and Rein, 1969:207).

The Training Center's research was aimed primarily toward the development of a concrete and appropriate training program for people employed in community corrections. Its initial investigation of needs for
training assisted in the development of pilot training sessions, which

in turn were examined in order to learn more about the type and methods of training that should be included in a training package for the succeeding year.

Whereas the exploration aims primarily at discovery through an inductive approach, demonstrations more clearly attempt to verify through measurement the relationship between the experimental variable (the program) and the dependent variables (specified outcomes or effects) through a deductive approach. Testing hypotheses is an appropriate approach to studying demonstrations. The focus on process is not restricted to learning how the program was carried out. In addition, efforts are made to determine whether the program was implemented in the intended or prescribed manner and to use program components or variables as possible causal explanations for the outcomes produced. For the Group Probation Project it was possible to test hypotheses related to the extent and nature of participation in groups with outcome on probation. The program was monitored to determine the manner in which it was implemented and to relate various aspects of the program to the success of the probation service in meeting its stated goals.

The extent to which there are strict controls on the program's operation and continual feedback of research findings is largely dependent on the nature and purpose of the evaluative study. For explorations, feeding back information from the evaluation to the program in order to affect both its objectives and procedures is of paramount importance. The Training Center relied on a constant feedback of information to plan the pilot project and then to use the lessons learned from the pilot project to develop a testable demonstration project for subsequent evaluation. Research and program development formed a dynamic and reciprocal process. On the other hand, if information is needed on the ultimate worth of program ideas, then a controlled situation is more likely to be insisted upon. And there would only be deliberate manipulation of program variables that have been predetermined for their contribution to the overall experiment. Additional demonstrations could be undertaken, prior to the formulation of a permanent program, to pursue insights and test changes that emerged from the initial research. The Group Probation Project, which sought information on the effectiveness of a particular approach, relied upon a controlled situation. Subsequent alterations in the program (such as working with the juveniles' families) were made only after the initial phase of the research was completed.

There has been considerable controversy about whether it is preferable to use in-house or outside evaluators. Inevitably, the answer is that there are distinct advantages and disadvantages to both. Since the research in the exploratory phase is an integral part of the program development, the project's own staff can take major responsibility for planning and conducting the research without having to fear accusations about bias. If needed, an external researcher would merely serve as a consultant, and his role would involve providing technical advice as needed.

Although initially hired as an outside evaluator for the Training Center, the researcher undertook regular staff responsibilities; and except for his more specific involvement in developing the research instruments, determining data collection procedures, and analyzing the data, his role was not distinctly different from that of other staff. On the other hand, in his involvement with the Group Probation Project, the researcher was clearly identified as an outside evaluator; and he acted like a watchdog, ready to oppose major alterations in program and procedures, for fear that they might render the evaluation useless.

Since there are somewhat different purposes for undertaking explorations and demonstrations, the acceptability of "soft" versus "hard" data varies somewhat according to the type of project. In the attempt to discover the nature of the program and its goals, explorations must rely to a greater extent on soft data, such as attitudes, felt needs, subjective estimates, and personal opinions. Much of the information collected by the Training Center was of this type. In testing demonstrations, however, where the outcome criteria are critically questioned, it is necessary to collect relatively objective data that can be assumed to have a known degree of reliability and validity. Although the Group Probation Project did include soft measures (such as attitudes toward the group), greater emphasis was placed on the collection of more objective data—demographic information, school grades and attendance, recidivism rates, and standardized self-concept scales.

There are not only differences in the research design used and the type of data collected for explorations and demonstrations, but the procedures and instruments for the collection of data are also somewhat different. Although both included administered questionnaires, the exploration relied more heavily on observation, unstructured interviews, and detailed notes.

Conclusion

This paper has emphasized the importance of evaluative research as an integral component for both explorations and demonstrations, particularly for its contribution to planning in criminal justice. In so doing, an attempt has been made to differentiate the purposes and, consequently, the appropriate research strategies for evaluating these projects. The research of explorations aimed to facilitate the process of conceptualizing and operationalizing "innovative" services into testable demonstrations. To increase the validity and generalizability of individual demonstration projects, replications in different places under varying conditions are needed. According to Joseph Wholey, however, many small studies have been carried out around the country that lack uniformity of design and objectives. Thus, results have rarely been comparable or responsive to the questions facing policy-makers (Wholey, 1971). To remedy this situation, there would be some merit in following Alice Rivlin's suggestion (1971) that funding organizations take the leadership in organizing, funding, and evaluating systematic experiments with various ways of implementing programs. Demonstration projects could then be planned in response to established priorities in the overall process of program development and/or policy-making while allowing for some random innovation.

References

Bailey, W. C.
   1966   Correctional outcome: an evaluation of 100 reports. Journal
           of Law, Criminology, and Police Science 57, no. 2: 153-60.
Buchanan, G. N., and J. S. Wholey
   1972   Federal level evaluation. Evaluation 1, no. 1: 17-22.
Eysenck, H.
   1961   Handbook of Abnormal Psychology. New York: Basic Books.
Fischer, J.
   1973   Is casework effective? a review. Social Work 18, no. 1:
           5-20.
Freeman, H. E., and C. C. Sherwood
   1971   Research in large-scale intervention programs. Pp. 262-76
           in Francis G. Caro, ed., Readings in Evaluation Research.
           New York: Russell Sage Foundation.
Marris, P., and M. Rein
   1969   Dilemmas of Social Reform. New York: Atherton.
Rivlin, A.
   1971   Systematic Thinking for Social Action. Washington, D.C.:
           Brookings Institute.
Suchman, E. A.
   1971   Action for what? a critique of evaluative research. Pp. 97-
           130 in Richard O'Toole, ed., The Organization, Manage-
           ment and Tactics of Social Research. Cambridge, Mass.:
           Schenkman.
Trow, M.
   1971   Methodological problems in the evaluation of innovation.
           Pp. 81-94 in Francis G. Caro, ed., Readings in Evaluation

        Research. New York: Russell Sage Foundation.
Wholey, J. C., et al.
    1971   Federal Evaluation Policy: Analyzing the Effects of Public
            Programs. Washington, D.C.: Urban Institute.

6

THE POLITICS
OF RESEARCH

James Boudouris

In 1973 U.S. Attorney General Elliot Richardson said, "We need to ask questions that start with what it is we are attempting to do, what we know about how to get there from here, how we know whether or not we are getting there from here, and whether or not we have arrived" (LEAA, 1973:2).

In other words, he was asking for a clear statement of objectives, a review of present knowledge, a monitoring of progress, and an evaluation of what was done. This is a basic outline for evaluative research. How this is to be done raises certain issues that must be dealt with in order to implement this policy. Some of the impediments to its implementation will be discussed in this paper.

The subject of evaluative research is closely tied to several areas of controversy among social scientists, some of which have only recently been raised and others of which are longer-standing. Whether speaking of evaluative research or policy research or applied research—and I will not distinguish among them—the discussion leads to differences of opinion regarding objective versus subjective data, qualitative versus quantitative studies, action versus research, and value-free versus value-oriented research (ASA, 1971). These conflicts are often underlaid by ideological commitments, such as liberals versus conservatives and traditionalists versus radicals. These controversies certainly are not confined to the social sciences, but reflect the ideological commitments of interest groups in our society. I will attempt to limit my paper to what LaMar Empey referred to as "the extra-scientific political realities that impinge upon research" (ASA, 1973b:5).

The academic training received by researchers has often been geared more for the survey of freshman sociology or psychology student attitudes, rather than the complex urban problems that compose law enforcement and criminal justice. At a recent conference for academic sociologists, the emphasis appeared to be on training nonacademic sociologists (that is, Ph. D. dropouts) without allowing this "to dilute the training standards for the discipline generally . . ." (ASA, 1973a:2; as summarized by H. Costner). On the contrary, I suggest that the universities need to upgrade their teaching of sociology and research methodology so that nonacademic sociologists (with or without Ph. D. s) can contribute relevant findings to the solution of the nation's social problems. But, at the same time, we should keep in mind Eric Hoffer's aphorism, "In human affairs every solution serves only to sharpen the problem, to show us more clearly what we are up against. There are no final solutions." (1968:144).

Some of the issues I will touch upon were discussed at the plenary sessions of the 1973 meeting of the American Sociological Association; but while I am considering issues related to research in the law enforcement and criminal justice systems, the plenary sessions dealt with the problems that arise in the conduct of research by social scientists for the presidential commissions on population, violence, crime and law enforcement, and obscenity and pornography. Extra-scientific political realities appear to impinge upon research dealing with any area of our lives. In Paul Lazarsfeld's comments on these papers, he outlined a plan for training sociologists in "applied sociology" or "the utilization of sociology" so that they can work in commission situations, agencies, or industry. His cirriculum includes reading case studies, internships in agencies and organizations, developing the ability to summarize and synthesize the literature, and having greater contacts with expert laymen.

The monitoring and evaluation of the functioning of our social institutions has been attempted only in relatively recent years. Federal funding of projects has only recently required that the projects be monitored and evaluated. But even with such requirements, there are various vested interests that resist evaluative research. The objectives of a program may be so ambiguous or multi-faceted that no real evaluation is possible, and the money allocated for the evaluation may be so small that it is merely window-dressing. In order to have an adequate evaluation of an innovative project, there must be data on a control or comparison group. To know whether the change introduced makes any difference, we must know how the agency or system operated before the innovation. Such data are usually lacking. Innovation without evaluation is a good public relations strategy but does not necessarily result in the improved functioning of an agency.

As soon as the researcher begins to collect data on the functioning of the agency or system, he encounters the "numbers games." In any bureaucratic system where the bureaucracy is reimbursed for alleged services to people—whether probationers, parolees, mental pa-

tients, or drug addicts—the accurate accounting of services and cases
is threatening to those who benefit from exaggerated claims. For
example, the total number of probationers serviced by an agency,
whether seen daily or monthly, for five minutes or one hour, represents a number of dollars reimbursable from the state and federal
governments. Drug addicts, or alleged drug addicts, receive a certain
number of dollars of public assistance; and the organization that is allegedly treating them, or rehabilitating them, receives a certain number of dollars from the state and federal governments. Exaggerated
numbers will bring the administrator and budget director more money
to work with, and more caseworkers and fewer cases per caseworker.
The researcher who strives for an accurate accounting can be deceived
or harrassed in countless ways when accuracy is irrelevant.

If the evaluation presents negative findings, the funding agency
is shown to have been a poor judge of what grant proposals to approve
. . . the caseworker is shown to be ineffective.

The truth apparently is not a comfortable cushion for bureaucrats
to sit on. Consequently, particularly in election years, police com-
missioners, who have been appointed by mayors, look for ways to re-
vise categories of crime statistics in order to show a decline in the
crime rates. Police departments have not employed researchers as
much as they have depended upon malleable statisticians.

As grant-renewal time approaches, the funded agency frantically
looks to the evaluators, not for research and objectivity but for public
relations propaganda. In fact, occasionally the two roles are joined
in the explicit title of director of public relations and research.

The rationalizations that have been employed for the spending of
the money by the funding and funded agencies have been of various
kinds: One can argue, "If the money isn't used for something, then the
Congress (or Legislature, or City Council) won't allocate as much next
time." Or, "If the money isn't given for these worthwhile humanitarian
causes out of the anti-crime funds, where else would we be able to get
it?"

The researcher is not asked for the facts because the facts take
time to collect; and, when they finally have been analyzed, the money
has been spent and the program either re-funded or scrapped, not on
the basis of evidence and carefully defined success criteria but on the
basis of argumentation, political manipulation, and verbal dexterity.
The decisions appear to be made on the basis of ideological commitments; and it is not by chance that the decision-makers are not the
criminologists and social scientists searching for the truth, but the
lawyers, politicians, and ex-advertising men whose skill is in persuad-
ing others to their point of view. The prevalence of lawyers also was
noted on the presidential commissions, and the conflicts between lawyers and social scientists was described.

There has been much rhetoric by governmental administrators about the need for research; but little has been funded, supported, or implemented. The need for evaluative research must be coupled with the current demand for "accountability" of our social institutions.

As in the protests of educators, this may only arouse more rationalizations. One defense mechanism is to redefine the goals. Teachers don't want to be held accountable for the reading and arithmetic scores of their students, but for "helping young people to develop their individual potential, teaching them how to make the democratic system work, fostering creativity, and aiding them in getting along with others." The police departments should not be expected to solve all of the society's ills, only to enforce the law. The courts see themselves not as arbitrators of the truth, but as uncloggers of the calendars.

When the system is composed of those who are more concerned with seniority, pay raises and promotions, status and prestige, more staff and larger budgets, bigger and newer facilities and equipment, and better images—then the questions to be examined are not what to do about crime, but what funds will produce the smallest change and disruption to the vested interests. Once everyone has become pacified to the point of returning to their individual spheres of irrelevance and opulence, the insanity of our society continues.

Research, the search for the truth, accountability—whatever terms we use—may bring our actions (and dollars) into a closer relationship with reality. The criteria to use must then become not profit, or how the bureaucracy can be maintained, but the purpose of the action and the expenditure of the funds, and how nearly the goals were achieved. In prisons, the issue should be what can be done to rehabilitate. In police departments, how much crime was reduced by what actions. In schools, how much the students were taught. In the courts, once a person has had his due process within the law, what constitutes a just outcome. In probation departments, what service was provided to whom, and its effectiveness and relevance to the probationers.

Research reports that lie on the shelves of libraries or in the bottom drawers of bureaucrats may just as well not be done. Community-action spokesmen who proclaim, "We don't need any more research! Give the money to the community instead!" are perhaps recognizing the lack of response to the research, rather than the quality of the research itself. The research findings must be redirected back into the system. But when the funds for the researcher come from the agency or institution that is being evaluated, the tenure of the researcher becomes problematic. He is faced with the conflicting goals of objective, evaluative research and the public image that the administrator hopes to preserve. If he chooses to write a report with regard only for the truth, he faces not having his grant renewed. If he tries to write a report to please the administrator, the interest groups, and the funding agencies, he has prostituted himself.

Marvin Wolfgang has discussed in detail the need for accountability of the criminal justice system, but what seems to me to remain problematic is to whom the criminal justice system is accountable and how this can be made a reality. Wolfgang states, "All parts of the criminal justice system should be accountable to the public at large, to the victim, and to the offender. Moreover, each subpart of the system should be accountable to the immediately preceding subpart" (1972: 16). The problem with the first part of that statement is that we are not given any suggestion on how this is to be implemented. The difficulty with the second part is that it might only lead to the bureaucratic game of passing the buck.

There are, I believe, ways to avoid these kinds of dilemmas. Part of the resolution of the conflicts could come from the willingness of bureaucrats to respond to evaluative research through change. The researcher, on the other hand, must be constantly searching for trade-offs and compromises with the bureaucrats. For example, the researcher may say to the administrator, "Give me access to your data and I will give you . . . what? change? policy? measures of success and failure?" Perhaps the administrator wants none of these things, only window-dressing, and that is the embittering moment for the researcher.

To avoid this, for a system of checks and balances to be established, the researcher's findings must be presented to regulatory bodies with the authority to implement them and to create changes within the criminal justice and law enforcement systems. The regulatory bodies must be debureaucratized and depoliticized for change to result.

Where federal funding is involved, the existing regulatory bodies are the Law Enforcement Assistance Administration and its research arm, the National Institute of Law Enforcement and Criminal Justice. In the dispensing of block grants to municipalities, the funding becomes increasingly bureaucratized and politicized as the block grants pass from the federal level to the state level to the local coordinating councils. In New York City, the Criminal Justice Coordinating Council, responsible for the allocation of federal funds to the criminal justice system of the city, is made up of seventy-four representatives from various segments of the community, but 46 percent are representatives of city or state agencies or political offices. On the executive committee, where the real decisions are made, 53 percent of the members may be classified as political or bureaucratic representatives (according to the 1973 Annual Report)—as is the mayor, who is chairman. On both the council and the executive committee, the largest professional group is the lawyers. None of the representatives are criminologists, social scientists, or researchers.

If criminal justice coordinating councils could be established that were not just vested-interest groups composed of representatives of vested-interest groups, they could serve as regulatory bodies responsible not just for funding purposes but also for the utilization of research findings so that criminal justice agencies could begin long-overdue reforms. These regulatory agencies would initiate evaluative research within the criminal justice system, not just monitor the results. Otherwise, as is the case now, any law enforcement or criminal justice agency that did not want to "make waves" would not need to apply for funds to evaluate its own effectiveness. The "accountability" of the criminal justice agencies would then be to such a regulatory body, and the function of the mass media would be to report on both the evaluative research and the organizational responses. Then each policeman, judge, probation officer, probationer, citizen, and taxpayer must accept personal responsibility for his response or lack of response to the truth. The pragmetic approach for all of us to take would be: What are we getting paid for?

It is my belief that the public has a right to know what proportion of arrests for what offenses in which precincts result in convictions. The public ought to know which judges make what sentencing decisions for which defendants, and what proportion of these defendants are back in court within six months or a year. The taxpayer has a right to know which probation officers see how many probationers, and with what results. The correctional institutions ought to inform the public as to what rehabilitative efforts were provided to which prisoners, and how successful they were when these persons were placed on parole. And, it seems to me, the parolees and probationers ought to know their chances of getting a job from what employers, what kind of assistance they are likely to get from their parole or probation officers, and what sort of rehabilitation is most likely to keep them from going through the system again.

References

American Sociological Association
     1971   Sociological research and public policy. American Sociologist 6, supp. iss. (June).

_____.
     1973a   Footnotes (February).

_____.
     1973b   Footnotes (August).
Hoffer, Eric
     1968   Aphorisms. In Calvin Tomkins, Eric Hoffer: An American

Odyssey. New York: E. P. Dutton.

Law Enforcement Assistance Administration
1973   Newsletter (August). Washington, D.C.: U.S. Government
         Printing Office.

Wolfgang, Marvin E.
1972   Making the criminal justice system accountable. Crime and
         Delinquency 18 (January): 15-22.

**ETHICAL ISSUES
IN EVALUATING
CRIMINAL JUSTICE
DEMONSTRATION PROJECTS**

Barry Krisberg and

Paul Takagi

Introduction

With the increase in LEAA funding, academic criminologists
have seen an increasing number of requests for proposals come across
their desks; most of these involve either planning or evaluation research
that is fairly easy to conceptualize, to design, and to suggest sampling
and measurement procedures. More often than not, the requests require the contractor to prepare a proposal in a matter of days; but in
some instances a more generous period of up to three weeks is provided. As a result, proposals are prepared with great haste, and in
the ensuing negotiations the research is discussed and clarified with
high-level officials in Washington or with officials of state or regional
criminal justice planning boards. Often the result is that research
procedures are employed that may violate ethical standards (as yet not
clearly defined by government or academic organizations that conduct
the bulk of this research) with respect to the use of human subjects,
especially the question of informed consent. But of equal concern is
the sorry fact that most of these proposals are prepared in a social
and political vacuum, in which the researcher often knows nothing
about the community in which the demonstration project is embedded.
This sociopolitical ignorance can have catastrophic consequences, because evaluations of criminal justice programs call for assessments
as well as recommendations and thus require the investigator to be
more than "technically" competent. Put bluntly, program evaluations
often have life-or-death consequences for the community and its members.

It is the purpose of this paper to present in narrative form the
authors' humbling experiences in an evaluative study of San Francisco's

Chinatown Youth Services and Coordinating Center, an LEAA-funded delinquency prevention project (Krisberg and Takagi, 1972). Our experiences were deeply affected by the ethical and political issues that emerged during the course of our research, and our aim is to illustrate the moral dilemmas that may be inherent in an evaluative study.

The Chinatown Youth Service Center

The logic underlying the Chinatown Youth Service Center was relatively simple, involving a diversion model supplemented with community-based services, such as individual counseling, group therapy, street work with gangs, and a twenty-four-hour residential treatment center for girls. The project director contacted the dean of the School of Criminology and asked if anyone on the faculty might like to evaluate the project. One of us called the director, and we met to discuss the details. There was approximately $22,000 available to do the evaluation, and the project staff needed to recommend the appropriate researchers. We were told that an agency in HEW had a "good deal of ego wrapped up in the idea of Youth Service Bureaus" and "The head of the agency has a special fondness for the Chinatown-North Beach Area."

We met with project staff and community people, and agreed to do an interim evaluation required by LEAA grant guidelines. We had ten days to do the fieldwork and seven days to write the final report. The board of managers of the project awarded the one-year evaluation grant to a private research organization that had a full year to study the project, whereas we had one month.[1]

Crime and Delinquency in Chinatown

The Chinatown Youth Service Center was begun in the summer of 1970 in response to a sudden and enormous increase in police arrests and citations of Chinese youngsters. In absolute numbers, there were 85 juvenile arrests and citations in 1964 and 442 in 1970, an increase of over 600 percent in seven years. Informed residents of the San Francisco Chinese community viewed these statistics as reflecting but the tip of an iceberg. Many told us, "There is much unreported crime in Chinatown. The problem is much larger than police or court figures show" (Fong-Torres, 1971). The community was concerned about the increasing volume of youth crime, but of greater concern was the increase in juvenile gang killings.

During the mid-1960s arrests by the police brought attention to
a group called "The Bugs," a gang of young Chinese burglars who
dressed completely in black and wore high-heeled boots and an upswept
hair style. The Bugs had burglarized forty-eight Chinatown businesses
and had extended their activities to the neighboring Russian Hill area,
a well-to-do white community. In 1965 the gang phenomenon again came
to public attention, but now its form was stylized violence reminiscent
of organized gangland slayings. This form of gang violence continued
and had claimed eighteen lives as of August 1973. In almost every case
the victims were shot in the head several times, sometimes in broad
daylight in front of 150 to 200 witnesses. Police were largely unable
to bring suspects to trial. In fact, some community residents felt that
the police were harassing large numbers of Chinese youth out of frustration over unproductive investigations. It thus appears that the
crime-free description of the Chinese community is largely fictional;
and we have been misled by a mythology constructed out of benign neg-
lect, racism, and poor research observations. One of our graduate
students uncovered California prison commitment statistics dating just
prior to the twentieth century that the Chinese in the 1890s had a prison
commitment rate of 38 per 10,000 population, compared with the white
rate of 10 per 10,000. The Chinese population declined after the turn
of the century largely as a result of restrictive immigration legislation.
Increases in departures accelerated especially when Chinese women
were discouraged from entering the United States. As late as the 1930s,
the Chinese-American community had a six ratio of eleven men to
one woman.

During the brief research period we spent a large proportion of
our time interviewing community leaders and knowledgeable informants,
subjecting them to intensive examination in order to determine the criteria by which we could measure the success or failure of the project.
Our task was not easy, because there was considerable disagreement
among those interviewed about the goals and objectives of the project.
Even among the board of managers, which served as the executive
body for the project, the scope of disagreement over desired project
ends was enormous.

The original proposal called for the establishment of a Youth Service Bureau with a youth advocacy unit that would attempt to divert
Chinese youngsters from juvenile court referrals. But many of the
people with whom we talked had something more in mind when they
thought of the project. Everyone we interviewed had uppermost in his
mind the gang problem, and some criticized the Youth Service Center
for using a diversion model that they felt was inappropriate for the
gang delinquency problem in Chinatown.

The director of the Center, a former probation officer and graduate of the Berkeley School of Criminology, had put together a series

of fairly traditional approaches to delinquency prevention, such as counseling, group sessions, and crisis intervention in the schools. The youth of the community asked that the Center develop a coffee house drop-in center, in response to a Center offer that "We have so much money, and such and such a place. What would you like to see happen to it and what will best serve you and your friends?" (Fong-Torres, 1972). The director of the project was trying to implement some of the principles of the Chicago Area Project, especially "the philosophy of youth involvement [it is to be emphasized] in every aspect of the program . . . from planning, to hiring [personnel], to implementation, and to the kinds of programs" (Fong-Torres, 1972). The director was successful in wringing a promise from the board of managers "not to sabotage any plans the youth come up with," and a promise to facilitate and help actualize the ideas.

The coffee house was to include an arts and crafts center, a twenty-four-hour counseling service, and English classes for newly arrived immigrants. These were the kinds of programs asked for by the street youth. The director and staff member did nightly street work to solicit interest and to maintain enthusiasm for the drop-in center.

One of the key members of the project, a former state parole agent and a lawyer, told us that he felt that the Chinatown project should focus upon younger children and stay away from the gangs. We learned later that this individual had received a beating, presumably from a gang; and this attack was interpreted by community leaders as a message by the gang to "lay off." Other community informants told us that the Center should be organized to offer direct services when these were requested by an individual or his family. Several community leaders cautioned us that a "professionally designed" program strategy would not solve the delinquency problem in Chinatown (Wang, 1971). Although everyone in the community was concerned about the gang killings, most were guarded in their discussions about the subject.

The only persons who felt that the project should do more street work with gangs were the well-known criminologist, mentioned earlier, and the two law enforcement officials, a police Juvenile Bureau chief and the chief of juvenile probation, who were members of the board of managers.

Our fieldwork had produced a clear picture of disagreements over the purpose of the Chinatown Youth Service Center. One of us had spent over a year researching a project working with violent gangs in an Eastern city; and that experience led him to conclude that without major changes in the political economy, gang violence would probably continue untouched by conventional approaches. As we continued our fieldwork and mulled over possible interpretations, we became increa-

singly apprehensive about the efforts of the director to reach the gangs
of Chinatown. This is what we wrote in our report:

> It is clear that the recent series of shootings and killings
> were important in terms of many individuals' definitions
> of Chinatown's "Youth Problem". It is important to note
> that both project staff and outside observers expressed
> doubts that doing conventional street work with gangs would
> be effective in reducing the apparently high level of inter-
> group violence. Many interviewees theorized that juvenile
> gangs in Chinatown are manifestations of the complex in-
> ternal structure of the Chinese community in San Francisco
> and that these gangs more nearly approximated organized
> crime than delinquency. From what little we understand
> about the social structure of Chinatown we would tentatively
> agree with the view expressed by some Center staff that
> their scarce resources should be directed towards work-
> ing with the younger siblings of gang members and others
> to deflect them from becoming gang members. It appears
> to us that until such time as indigenous leaders decide to
> control the gang problem and agree to actively work
> towards that end, the street shootings and killings are
> likely to continue (Krisberg and Takagi, 1972:6-7).

In our recommendations we included a section about the project directorship that reflected our feelings on an obviously dangerous situation.
We recommended the following:

> The director of the Center cannot alone make decisions
> that affect the staff, the clients, and ultimately relations
> within and outside of Chinatown. This is too much to ask
> of a director as a responsibility, and more importantly,
> the consequences can be enormous. We believe that the
> director of the Center by virtue of his position is not only
> a professional but a political decision-maker as well. In
> view of this, we recommend the establishment of an execu-
> tive decision-making committee . . . (Krisberg and
> Takagi, 1972:20).

Our evaluation report was turned over to the Center on May 2,
1973. On June 26, 1973, the director of the Center, Barry Fong-
Torres, was chatting with a friend in his apartment, when someone
rang the doorbell. Moments after he opened the door, five shots were
fired, bullets striking him in the head, eye, mouth, and chest. He died
almost instantly.[2] A few days later, at a press conference, a high

elected official of San Francisco, although appalled by the killings, minimized them in reassuring white people that it was safe for them to go into Chinatown because all of the murder victims had been Chinese.

Criminology, Program Research, and Professional Morality

We were deeply shaken by the death of Barry Fong-Torres, whom we had known to be a deeply committed and humane individual. We reviewed our report, the field notes, the taped interviews, and other data to determine if our evaluation activities had in any way precipitated the tragedy or whether there were any clues that the director's life was in danger. The only thing we could identify was the vague and uneasy feeling that the situation was dangerous, which we had indicated in our report.

We are not suggesting that criminologists are the only culpable ones in the tragedies that result from social programs. But all too often it is the academic and professional community that devises new project ideas, sells these packages to politicians and funding agencies or, more subtly, remains silent on their worthless or even harmful effects. Neither do we suggest that criminologists pack their bags. Rather, we urge our colleagues to practice their knowledge when dealing with communities concerned about delinquency and crime problems. For instance, we know that the history of delinquency prevention has been grossly disappointing. From the 1926 study by Sheldon and Eleanor Glueck of Judge Baker's Child Guidance Clinic to the highly sophisticated and elaborate study by Lamar T. Empey and Steven G. Lubeck in the Silverlake Experiment, not a single delinquency project has been able to demonstrate the achievement of programmatic goals. "Success" stories printed in the literature turn out to be little more than program huckstering through the use of pseudo-scientific research designs. This clearly means that delinquency prevention, including diversion projects, is not a viable enterprise, or that our research methodology is not yet capable of yielding fruitful results.

Theory and Community Practice

The bulk of the delinquency prevention programs consist of individually oriented approaches to education and treatment, which are more or less variations on themes introduced into the criminological literature by William Healy and August Aichhorn at the turn of the twentieth century. These programs assume that the delinquent is sick, unsocialized, or inadequate, and that through intervention by the state, the delinquent may be redeemed. Such efforts continue to be designed and funded, despite the criticism by communities and clients who do not see themselves as pathological or inferior. Programs of this sort are attractive because they deflect attention from problems of the social structure.

Indeed, criminologists familiar with the history of delinquency prevention in the United States know that few, if any, granting agencies or universities have sponsored projects that openly seek to correct the poverty, racism, and internal colonization that foster and maintain Chinatowns and similar communities throughout America. "The recent demise of extra-murally funded projects in ghetto communities from East Oakland on the West Coast to Bedford Stuyvesant on the East Coast makes very clear the distinction between projects designed to control the 'dangerous classes' and those that are abruptly terminated because they threaten existing political and economic relations" (Krisberg, 1972:128).

Lacking the firm knowledge that would allow us to make constructive recommendations, we can only rely upon our experiences and our biases. Through rather different professional and life experiences, we have reached a consensus that our bias lies with community-controlled approaches to delinquency prevention. This conclusion is based, in part, upon our knowledge about the failure of more conventional approaches to delinquency prevention; but more persuasive is the accumulated body of research findings that indicate that more than any other variables, poverty and racism contribute to the victimization we label "delinquency." Because of our bias we recommended in our evaluation of the Chinatown Youth Center that the feasibility of establishing a community-controlled effort be explored.

A number of community-controlled efforts are being attempted throughout America: free medical examinations, mini-schools, escort services for the elderly in ghetto communities, and drug abuse control centers. It may come as a surprise to some, but groups such as the Black Panthers, La Raza Unida, RAP in San Francisco, and the Community Concern 13 in Philadelphia are actively seeking to reduce delinquency and crime through such programs.

Criminologists have not studied the efforts of these groups for various reasons. First, these groups are not generally funded by extra-mural grants and, therefore, there is no money to do evaluation studies. Second, these groups probably would reject the attempt of criminologists from outside the community to study neighborhood residents without some concrete payoff for their people. Third, government agencies and law enforcement officials often are openly hostile to these groups and would prefer that they not be portrayed positively.

Students of delinquency, despite the problems mentioned above, need to move out into the communities to understand the relationship between crime, social injustice, and racism. We must study the effects of systems of internal colonization that may have stripped some of our minority communities of the ability to handle local problems. We need to understand how selective processes within the superstructure force members of the community to adapt to the techno-economic environment in deviant and socially harmful ways.

Finally, we believe that criminologists have a professional and moral responsibility to aid criminal justice workers in seeing the vacuousness of conventional approaches to delinquency prevention and control. We need to understand that it is no accident that poor people and people of color are the principal clients of the criminal justice system and the principal victims of its injustices.

Notes

1. At the time of our discussions with the Youth Service Center staff, we were unwilling to commit ourselves to do a large-scale study upon a project that appeared too simple to warrant a $22,000 one-year study.

2. A note was found near the body warning "Pig Informers Die Young." This note suggested to many that gang members were responsible for the shooting.

References

Fong-Torres, B.
   1971   Narrative description. San Francisco: Chinatown Youth
           Services and Coordinating Center. Unpublished paper.
_____.
   1972   Letter to Robert Foster, Youth Development and Delinquency
           Prevention Administration, HEW, Washington, D.C. (January 5).
Krisberg, B.
   1972   The gang and the community. Berkeley: University of California (December). Unpublished paper.
Krisberg, B. and P. Takagi
   1972   Evaluation of the Chinatown Youth Services and Coordinating
           Center. Berkeley: University of California (May). Unpublished paper.

Lan, D.
    1969   Report of the San Francisco Chinese Community Citizens'
              Survey and Fact Finding Committee. San Francisco: H. J.
              Carle.

_____.

    1971   The Chinatown sweatshops: oppression and an alternative.
              Amerasia Journal 1, no. 3 (November): 40-57.
Shaffer, A.
    1971   The Cincinnati social unit experiment. Social Services Re-
              view 45, no. 2 (June): 159-72.
Wang, L.
    1971   An interview with L. Ling Chi Wang. In Amy Tachiki et al.,
              eds., Roots: an Asian American Reader. Los Angeles:
              Continental Graphics.
Warren, M.
    1972   Correctional Treatment in Community Settings, a Report of
              Current Research. Washington, D.C.: U.S. Government
              Printing Office.
Witmer, H., and E. Tufts
    1954   The Effectiveness of Delinquency Prevention Programs.
              Washington, D.C.: U.S. Government Printing Office.

8

SOCIAL SCIENCE RESEARCH IN THE AFTERMATH OF *FURMAN v. GEORGIA:* CREATING NEW KNOWLEDGE ABOUT CAPITAL PUNISHMENT IN THE UNITED STATES

Hugo Adam Bedau

The Furman Decision and Its Impact

In June 1972 the Supreme Court announced its decision in Furman v. Georgia and related cases (408 U.S. 238-470). The Court ruled that the death penalty was unconstitutional as currently administered, with trial judges and juries having unguided discretion to sentence to death or life, because it violated the Eighth and Fourteenth Amendments as a "cruel and unusual punishment." Future historians may well be able to show this decision to be the watershed in the nation's long-standing controversy over capital punishment. It was especially noteworthy for the way in which complex and varied social science evidence had been presented in the briefs and arguments by the attorneys on behalf of their death row clients (see Meltsner, 1973). As the Court's opinions showed, this evidence carried persuasive effect and provided the basic foundation for the decision.

Although many of the data accumulated found their way into the nine separate and diverse opinions written in this case, it was the showing of infrequency, arbitrariness, and discrimination in the administration of the death penalty that held together the five Justices who formed the majority. Mr. Justice Douglas observed, "One searches our chronicles in vain for the execution of any member of the affluent strata of this society" (253-54). Mr. Justice Stewart commented that those under sentence of death in the United States were "a capriciously selected random handful" (309-10). Mr. Justice White continued the same objection when he wrote, "There is no meaningful basis for distinguishing the few cases where [the death penalty] . . . is imposed from the many cases where it is not" (313). Justices Brennan and Marshall concurred in these findings and also stressed a different

objection: ". . . the threat of death has no greater deterrent effect than
the threat of imprisonment" (Brennan, 302); "capital punishment cannot be justified on the basis of its deterrent effect" (Marshall, 354).
This is but a sampling from a great wealth of dicta in Furman that
shows how the social science evidence offered to the Court managed to
have a powerful impact upon its reasoning.

Impressive as the ruling in Furman was, however, it was clear
that it did not directly settle the issue of whether the death penalty has
any place in our society. Although eight of the nine Justices indicated
a personal opposition to capital punishment, only five—a bare majority—
agreed that the death penalty as then administered violated the Constitution, and only two maintained that the death penalty in any form would
be unconstitutional. Even though the prevailing discretionary use of
capital punishment was entirely repudiated, there was room in the
Furman ruling for new experiments with the death penalty, possibly
as a mandatory punishment or possibly as a discretionary punishment
with clear statutory guidelines for trial juries to follow. Important
though these possibilities were, they had not been placed squarely before the Court in the Furman litigation, and in characteristic fashion
the Court left them undecided.

Furthermore, although the effect of social scientific evidence
upon the Court's thinking was clearly evident, and while all the Court
agreed on the relevance of factual evidence to the legal issues, several
of the dissenting Justices openly complained of the paucity and insufficiency of evidence. Chief Justice Burger was especially outspoken
on this issue. "Data of more recent vintage is essential," he wrote at
one point (390). He said of the majority Justices that "they share a
willingness to make sweeping factual assertions, unsupported by empirical data. . ." (405). Quite apart from the question of whether such
objections are well founded, they are now part of the record of the Supreme Court's assessment of the data base used to attack the death
penalty; and such doubts and objections will not be dissipated of their
own accord.

There are several results, then, of the Furman decision. It ir-
revocably abolished the prevailing mode of inflicting the death penalty.
It defined the factual issues on which the future of the death penalty
would eventually be determined. These issues include the deterrent
effect of mandatory death penalties, the acceptability to the public of
mandatory executions for whole classes of criminals, and the arbitrary
and discriminatory results under nominally mandatory death penalties.
On these and other empirical questions, "data of recent vintage" will
undoubtedly prove decisive in the months and years immediately ahead,
provided they can be properly assembled by imaginative researchers
and then marshaled effectively by lawyers experienced in the use of
social science data in a legal setting.

Confronting the Need for Research

In October 1972 the NAACP Legal Defense and Educational Fund
sponsored a conference in New York and brought together two dozen
leading researchers and scholars who had wide familiarity with empirical research on sociological, psychological, demographical, historical, and other questions relating to correction and the administration
of criminal justice. At this conference Anthony Amsterdam and Jack
Himmelstein, the two lawyers chiefly responsible for the anti-death
penalty litigation since 1967, made clear the interests of courts in further objective social science research on all aspects of the death penalty. It became evident to all at the conference that the first priority
was the systematic exploration of the feasibility of coordinated social
science research into the area of capital punishment, which would en-
list the participation, so far as possible, of investigators around the
nation and from all the relevant disciplines. In February 1973 funding
for this investigation was sought and obtained from the Russell Sage
Foundation by this writer (Bedau, 1973a).

During the spring and summer of 1973, a series of interrelated
activities were organized to accomplish this project. One of the major
instruments conceived and executed during this period was a series of
conferences arranged at several of the leading centers of social science
research in criminology and criminal justice, to bring together pro-
spective researchers and lawyers informed on the legally relevant issues needing research. These conferences were conducted at the
Center for Studies in Criminology and Criminal Justice, University of
Pennsylvania; the Center for the Study of Law and Society, University
of California, Berkeley; the Center for Research in Criminal Justice,
University of Illinois, Chicago Circle; the Department of Criminology,
Florida State University; the Center for the Study and Reduction of Violence, UCLA Medical School; and the Center for Criminal Justice, Harvard Law School. More than 100 graduate students, faculty, and other
researchers attended these conferences by invitation. Two other conferences were arranged to deal with specific areas in which any further
research was known to require extensive prior review and investigation:
on deterrence, at Yale Law School, and on survey research, at the
Russell Sage Foundation offices in New York.

Meanwhile, in the months after <u>Furman,</u> the urgency for undertaking this research was being underlined by political events. In July
1972, at a press conference, President Richard Nixon indicated his
belief that the death penalty was the appropriate punishment for certain
crimes. In November 1972 the voters of California passed Proposition
17, to restore a mandatory death penalty for several crimes and to
prevent judicial review of such legislation. In the same month the

Gallup Poll reported that 57 percent of the adult public supported the
death penalty in some form for various crimes. In December the Florida Legislature, in special session, adopted into law several new
death penalty statutes. The National Association of Attorneys General
voted a resolution to recommend the mandatory death penalty in certain
cases. In January 1973 Attorney General Richard Kleindienst informed
the press that the Nixon administration intended to ask Congress to pass
legislation for mandatory death penalties covering several categories
of crimes. Within a year after Furman, commissions had been formed
in several states to make recommendations on the issue; and bills to
restore capital punishment had been introduced in three dozen state
legislatures. By midsummer such bills had already been signed into
law in twenty states. On the second anniversary of Furman, twenty-
eight states had new death penalty legislation and more than 100 persons in seventeen states had been sentenced to death under these new
laws (Kendall, 1974). Although the de facto moratorium on executions
continued (there has been no execution since June 1967), it was clear
that the nation was still a long way from totally abolishing the death
penalty.

Thus, in the aftermath of Furman, the resources of the social
science community had been explored and organized with respect to
kinds of research relevant to the future of the death penalty. Concur-
rently, in the political arena, statutes had been passed in many jurisdictions to restore the death penalty, framed so as to avoid the thrust
of the Supreme Court's decision in Furman. This guaranteed a further
round of litigation on the constitutionality of capital punishment, as
well as debate in the legislatures over the merits of new capital statutes
and agonizing appraisals by the chief executives over particular executions.

Developing the Research Agenda

Three kinds of empirical evidence might have sufficed, had they
been available, to stem the tide of public and legislative backlash to
Furman. One would be a showing that many of those sentenced for capital crimes in recent years were in fact innocent. Another would be
conclusive evidence that the death penalty is not a deterrent (or not as
good a deterrent as imprisonment, or that the use of capital punishment
incited more violence than it prevented). The third would be that all
capital offenders are one-time criminals, and can be imprisoned and
paroled without danger to others. No evidence to support these extreme
hypotheses has been forthcoming, and none is likely. They are mentioned here only to indicate that the brush fire of legislative reimpo-

sitions of capital punishment since <u>Furman</u> could have been prevented and controlled, if at all, only by social science evidence of a stunning and unprecedented nature. Any new increments to our knowledge about capital punishment less striking and less conclusive than this would be, as they have been, simply swept aside or ignored in the rush to restore statutory authority to execute murderers and other criminals.

On the other hand, these extreme hypotheses do provide suggestions for the ideal research agenda. Miscarriages of justice, deterrence, and the criminal histories of capital offenders had been studied during the 1960s and the results had proved to be relevant to the decision in <u>Furman</u>. Any future legislative and judicial action on capital punishment would no doubt be influenced by further empirical findings on these topics. However, since there was no reason to expect novel empirical findings in regard to any of these matters, and since they were essentially unrelated issues, they could not form the nucleus of the research agenda, nor could they be relied upon to give it structure and coherence. Another approach was needed.

Conceived in the abstract, one might suppose that the ideal research agenda on the death penalty in the post-<u>Furman</u> era would be governed by four major considerations. First, one would distinguish the empirically untestable from the empirically testable issues affecting the administration and effects of capital punishment, and attend only to the latter set of propositions. One of the difficulties in the constitutional argument culminating in <u>Furman</u> was to determine which hypotheses relevant to the prohibition of "cruel and unusual punishment" really were empirically testable and which were not. A study of the briefs (Legal Defense Funds, 1971) and of previous arguments by others on the Eighth Amendment issues (Gottlieb, 1961; Goldberg and Dershowitz, 1970) shows that little or none of the empirical evidence available to the courts for interpretation was systematically undertaken by social science investigators with Eighth Amendment issues in mind. Instead, the attorneys who argued against the constitutionality of the death penalty were required to adapt the available empirical evidence as best they could. Odd as it may seem, in 1970 there was little or nothing in print to guide empirically oriented lawyers as to what issues were at stake in Eighth Amendment arguments over capital (or any other mode of) punishment.

Second, one would distinguish between the empirical hypotheses relating the forms of capital punishment that the Supreme Court in <u>Furman</u> had specifically rejected, and those empirical hypotheses that concerned aspects of the death penalty that the Court left unresolved in <u>Furman</u>. It was empirical issues of the latter sort that were most in need of attention from social science investigators, since the holding in <u>Furman</u> was not likely to be reversed. Two major topics on which future research should focus were quickly identified. One had to do with actual or likely administration of "mandatory" death penalties. Such

statutes had prevailed throughout the nation a century ago, and the doz-
en or so that survived were not invalidated by Furman. New death penalty legislation, therefore, was very likely to take this form. The other
had to do with actual or likely administration of death penalty statutes
with "guided discretion," whereby after conviction for a capital crime,
the defendant's sentence to death or to life would depend on whether the
court found, respectively, any "aggravating" or any "mitigating" circumstances. In 1972 no capital statutes of this sort existed, and the
ruling in Furman suggested they might be acceptable to the Supreme
Court. Short of a constitutional amendment to overturn the holding in
Furman—an unlikely eventuality—all new empirical research projects
that would have maximum policy relevance would be addressed to the
death penalty administered in one of these two ways.

Third, one would want to distinguish those empirical issues on
which new information might be obtained by research and that probably
would not influence either legislatures or courts from those that might
yield hypotheses relevant to the inquiries of such groups. Again, one
would set aside the former group of issues as undeserving of the scarce
time and money available.

Finally, one would attempt to choose from among the latter set
those empirically testable hypotheses about capital punishment that,
because of their relation to other issues in social science, criminology,
and the administration of criminal justice, would be likely to arouse
the curiosity of competent investigators and command the attention of
funding sources.

These four second-order considerations provided the essential
guidelines for constructing the ideal research agenda on capital punishment in the post-Furman era.

Research Actually Proposed and Initiated

There was, however, a profound difficulty in hoping to undertake
a research agenda guided by such criteria. The issues and hypotheses
that such criteria would isolate had no likelihood of being transformed
into research projects and then implemented without strong central
leadership from a research director. Such centrality of direction would
be impossible without substantial funding and discretion in its use.
Those interested in initiating a program of relevant social science research on capital punishment recognized these contingencies. By the
autumn of 1973, efforts were under way to fund a capital punishment
research project with a three-to-five-year duration and an annual budget of $150,000. The bid for these funds during 1973-74 failed.

This was to some extent anticipated; and from the onset smaller
research eggs were placed in several different baskets, in the hope
they would hatch separately. An ever-present imponderable was the
rate at which the new death penalty cases would reach the Supreme

Court. Any new social science evidence was better than none; and if
the ideal research agenda could be implemented only with the availabil-
ity of unprecedentedly large sums of money, then it was vital that projects not in need of funding (and however low on the priority list) be
initiated anyway, lest the new round of appellate litigation be forced to
get under way without any support from post-Furman empirical research.

All these factors were constantly weighed during 1973, and the
result at midyear was shown in a report submitted to the Russell Sage
Foundation (Bedau and Currie, 1973). That report contained seven
proposed research projects by as many different teams of researchers.[1]
By the end of that summer, the list of potential investigations had increased to twenty-five (Bedau, 1973b). At that time it was still hoped
that all these separate projects would in due course be winnowed, supplemented, and integrated in one large overall research project with
central management and funding.

While it is true that each of these twenty-five projects was to
some extent guided by the fourfold set of criteria outlined above, it is
also true that, taken as a whole, they formed an ad hoc set and would
yield rather less than the ideally relevant results. Yet these twenty-
five projects did represent the genuine interests and competencies of
interested researchers in a wide range of social science fields. In that
sense they did constitute a genuine measure of the prospects for death
penalty research during the mid-1970s. What these hypotheses and issues may have lacked as an agenda for research when measured by an
ideal criterion, they probably did possess if measured by the practical
realities of the academic marketplace. It must be added, however, that
most of these projects, and probably all of the dozen or so most valuable, were doomed to remain paper dreams until funding was sought
and found in each individual case.

One year after Furman, therefore, it is hardly surprising that
none of the substantial research from this ad hoc agenda was under
way, except for the few projects that required no special fund-raising
efforts. Two years after Furman, many of the original projects had
been shelved indefinitely for lack of funding. (Fortunately, other research projects had meanwhile been identified, and interested investigators were undertaking the preliminary development of research
proposals for them.) Of the original twenty-five research proposals
identified in 1973, only two had been funded by mid-1974. One was the
project undertaken by a group of social psychologists working at Stanford University to develop a new survey research instrument sensitive
to the post-Furman legislative options. During the winter of 1973-74,
the Russell Sage Foundation supported the development of the instrument and its administration to a California sample (Ellsworth, Ross,
and Amsterdam, 1974). The second was a project directed out of the

University of Pennsylvania to study the effects of sentencing in three
jurisdictions (District of Columbia, Massachusetts, New York) before
and after the shift from mandatory to discretionary death sentencing
(Wolfgang, 1972). This project was funded by the Ford Foundation on
the second anniversary of Furman. This research will test whether
"mandatory" death penalties really eliminate discretion or arbitrariness, or only shift it from the sentencing phase to earlier stages in
the judicial process—for instance, by allowing the prosecutor to plea-
bargain or by encouraging the jury to convict for a lesser offense.

Early in 1974, following a symposium on capital punishment at
the annual meeting of the Orthopsychiatric Association, the decision
was made to devote an issue of American Journal of Orthopsychiatry
early in 1975 to some of the new social science research results on the
death penalty. Several new projects, including some that required
special funding, were set in motion by the prospect of this special journal issue.

Evaluation of New Research

In the two years since Furman, the research on capital punishment brought to completion and published is only a small fraction of
what is under way and to be published within the next two years. Space
does not permit a thorough evaluation of that literature, though mention
at least should be made of several documents, books, and articles.

1. One might have thought that with several dozen states contem-
plating new death penalty legislation, a series of well-financed investigations into relevant factual issues would have been mounted by
legislative study commissions. The contrary seems to be true. The
only exception is the report prepared by the special study commission
in Pennsylvania (Packel, 1973). It is of interest to social scientists
because of the seven staff reports it contains, some of which undertake
research in new areas and most of which address themselves to aspects
of the issue of mandatory death sentencing. [2]

2. There are several recent books on capital punishment, but
only one of them contains any new research of interest to social scientists (Bowers, 1974). Apart from reprinting in two of its chapters pre-
Furman research done by others (Fattah, 1972; Wolfgang, 1972; see
also Wolfgang and Riedel, 1973), Bowers' book contains some evidence
of "recent vintage," as requested by Chief Justice Burger in his dissent
in Furman. Much of it is derived from scrutinizing data originally collected by others (Teeters and Zibulka, 1966) that hitherto have been
neglected. The two most original chapters are those in which Bowers
studies the deterrent effects of the shift from mandatory to discretion-

ary death penalties, and of the nationwide moratorium on executions since 1967, using the Teeters-Zibulka data and other standard data sources. His chief conclusion is this: "There is no evidence in the foregoing analysis that the moratorium on executions in the United States contributed to increasing the level of homicide in this country nor that the mandatory application of the death penalty had any greater deterrent effectiveness than its discretionary use. The evidence is remarkably consistent (Bowers, 1974:158).

3. Less than a year after Furman, releases by the Harris Survey showed a new level of public support for the death penalty: 59 percent for, 31 percent against, 10 percent uncertain (Harris, 1973). Mandatory capital punishment, however, was not supported by a majority for any crime, although 41 percent did support it for the killing of a policeman (Harris, 1973). No test was made of the interesting evidence reported elsewhere, based on a Canadian sample, that many support the death penalty even if they do not believe that it is a superior deterrent (Vidmar, 1973). In another essay that critically examines all the survey research on capital punishment, the authors conclude that more subtle measures of public opinion need to be developed and that the typical Gallup, Roper, and NORC polls, which have been "limited to an examination of general abstract statements of support for, or opposition to, capital punishment, do not provide adequate information" (Vidmar and Ellsworth, 1974:1269-70).

4. The death penalty in America has never totally lacked the attention of professional historians; but there is a dearth of dissertations, monographs, and other historical studies, and nothing to compare with the great treatise by L. Radzinowicz (1948). Lately, however, we have begun to receive a series of shorter papers that promise to increase our understanding of our past (Mackey, 1973, 1974b). The most important contribution to date from these new investigations may be the evidence unearthed about attitudes a century ago toward the then prevalent mandatory death penalty: "Antebellum Americans . . . whose experience with mandatory capital punishment was extensive, tended to account it a dangerous failure. They were satisfied that mandatory capital punishment did indeed have a deterrent effect; it deterred jurors from convicting palpably guilty men" (Mackey, 1974a:35). Whether we shall reexperience the phenomenon of jury nullification in capital cases in the 1970s remains to be seen. No doubt, however, a closer study of our own past has much to teach us.

Conclusion

The exact relationship between social science research and public policy formation by legislatures and courts remains something of

a mystery. This is true whether the policy is formed by the legislature
or the courts, and whether it is determined at the state or the federal
level. It is undeniable, however, that the general skepticism toward
capital punishment, not to mention the categorical hostility toward it
among so many, is a result of the social science research on the history, the law, and the effects of executions in this country. As we have
seen earlier, the Supreme Court's momentous decision in Furman v.
Georgia showed that the nation's highest tribunal would not only take
judicial notice of the results of social science research on this issue,
but even ask for more. There is every reason to believe that this
will continue to be true in the future. The relevance, therefore, of
policy-oriented social science research on the unanswered questions
regarding capital punishment is incontestable. In due course, history
will show whether the social science community prosecutes with vigor
the empirical studies necessary to increase our knowledge of this subject, and whether our governments will respond to that knowledge.

Notes

    1. The proposed projects and the principal investigators were as
follows: "Public Attitudes Toward the Death Penalty" (Neil Vidmar,
Yale Law School); "Change from Mandatory to Discretionary Death
Penalties" (William Bowers, Northeastern University); "Patterns of
Prison Homicides" (Peter Buffum, Pennsylvania Prison Society);
"Legislative Reimposition of the Death Penalty" (Edward Bronson and
Charles Price, Ohio State University); "Differential Imposition of the
Death Penalty for Rape" (Marvin Wolfgang and Marc Riedel, Univer-
sity of Pennsylvania); "The Death Penalty as an Inciter of Violence"
(William Graves, M.D., and Alan Kringel, M.D.); "A Cost/Benefit
Study of the Death Penalty" (Ronald Slivka).
    2. By title and investigator, these studies were as follows: "The
Effect of Mandatory and Discretionary Death Sentences on Commuta-
tions and Executions, 1915-1962" (Marc Riedel); "A Review of the Lit-
erature Contrasting Mandatory and Discretionary Systems of Sentencing
Capital Cases" (John McCloskey); "A Study of Capital Sentencing of
First Degree Murderers in Pennsylvania" (Marc Riedel); "Homicides
in Pennsylvania Prisons, 1964-1973" (Peter Buffum); "Capital Punishment: A Deterrent for Major Crime?" (Richard Pakola and Robert
Sadoff); "A Report on the Questionnaire Administered to Life Term Inmates at State Correctional Institution, Graterford" (Marc Riedel); "A
Content Analysis of Public Hearings of the Governor's Study Commission on Capital Punishment" (Marc Riedel). Several of these papers

have been revised for publication in a special issue on capital punishment of <u>Prison Journal</u>, Volume 53, Number 1 (Spring-Summer), 1974.

References

Bedau, H. A.
  1973a   The future of capital punishment—a problem for law and the
          social sciences. A proposal submitted to the Russell Sage
          Foundation (January).
  1973b   An inventory of death penalty research projects. A supple-
          mentary report to the Russell Sage Foundation (August).
Bedau, H. A., and E. Currie
  1973   Social science research and the death penalty in America.
          An interim report submitted to the Russell Sage Foundation
          (June).
Bowers, W. J., ed.
  1974   Executions in America. Lexington, Mass.: D. C. Heath
          and Co.
Ellsworth, P., L. Ross, and A. Amsterdam
  1974   Investigation of empirical issues related to capital punish-
          ment. A proposal submitted to the Russell Sage Foundation
          (January).
Fattah, E. A.
  1972   A Study of the Deterrent Effect of Capital Punishment with
          Special Reference to the Canadian Situation. Ottawa: De-
          partment of the Solicitor General.
Goldberg, A. J., and A. M. Dershowitz
  1970   Declaring the death penalty unconstitutional. Harvard Law
          Review 83 (June): 1773-1819.
Gottlieb, G. H.
  1961   Testing the Death Penalty. South California Law Review 34
          (Spring): 268-81.
Harris, L.
  1973   The Harris Survey (June 11, June 14).
Kendall, D. E.
  1974   Memorandum on Death Row U.S.A. (June 18, 1974) NAACP
          Legal Defense Fund.
Legal Defense Fund
  1971   Briefs for Petitioners: Aikens v. California; Furman v.
          Georgia; Jackson v. Georgia. New York: NAACP Legal De-
          fense and Educational Fund.
Mackey, P. E.
  1973   Edward Livingston on the punishment of death. Tulane Law
          Review 48 (December): 25-42.

1974a   The inutility of mandatory capital punishments: an historical
         note. Boston University Law Review 54 (January): 32-35.
1974b   "The result may be glorious"—anti-gallows movement in
         Rhode Island 1838-1852. Rhode Island History 33 (February):
         19-31.

Meltsner, M.
1973   Cruel and Unusual: The Supreme Court and Capital Punish-
         ment. New York: Random House.

Packel, I. (Chairman)
1973   Report of the Governor's Study Commission on Capital Pun-
         ishment. Harrisburg: Commonwealth of Pennsylvania (Sep-
         tember).

Radzinowicz, L.
1948   A History of English Criminal Law. Vol. I, The Movement
         for Reform. London: Stevens and Sons.

Teeters, N. K., and C. J. Zibulka
1966   Executions under state authority—an inventory. Pp. 200-
         401 in William J. Bowers, ed., Executions in America.
         Lexington, Mass.: D. C. Heath and Co.

Vidmar, N.
1973   Retribution motives and other correlates of Canadian atti-
         tudes toward the death penalty. A paper presented to the
         annual meeting of the Canadian Psychological Association
         (June).

Vidmar, N., and P. Ellsworth
1974   Public opinion and the death penalty. Stanford Law Review
         26 (June): 1245-70.

Wolfgang, M. E.
1972   Statement submitted before Subcommittee No. 3, Committee
         on the Judiciary, House of Representatives, 92nd Congress,
         2nd Session (March 16). Pp. 172-89 in Capital Punishment,
         Hearings on H. R. 8414 etc. Washington, D.C.: U.S. Go-
         vernment Printing Office.

Wolfgang, M. E., and M. Riedel
1973   Race, judicial discretion, and the death penalty. The An-
         nals American Academy of Political and Social Science 407
         (May): 119-33.

9

A PRIVATE OMBUDSMAN
FOR A PUBLIC AGENCY:
PLANNING AND DEVELOPMENT
OF THE CONNECTICUT
CORRECTIONAL SYSTEM OMBUDSMAN

Brian L. Hollander

In the report of the President's Commission on Law Enforcement and Administration of Justice, The Challenge of Crime in a Free Society, there is only a light reference to the role of an ombudsman in the administration of criminal justice. In a general discussion of grievance mechanisms, an ombudsman is identified as "only one possible model— [to assist] citizens in understanding and dealing with the many official agencies that affect their lives" (President's Commission, 1967:282). No mention is made of the ombudsman in the section of the report dealing with corrections.

By 1973, with the release of the Corrections Report of the National Advisory Commission on Criminal Justice Standards and Goals, the conclusion that ombudsmen should be inserted into the correctional process apparently had gained widespread support. The Commission took the position that every correctional agency should have the services of an ombudsman. The role is described as follows:

> . . . hear complaints of employees or inmates who feel aggrieved by the organization or its management, or (in the case of inmates) who feel aggrieved by employees or the conditions of their incarceration. Such an Ombudsman would be roughly analogous to the inspector general in the military and would require substantially the same degree of authority to stimulate changes, ameliorate problem situations, and render satisfactory responses to legitimate problems. The Ombudsman should be located organizationally in the office of the top administrator (National Advisory Commission, 1973:459).

The obvious question raised by these seemingly disparate positions is why the significant change in attitude regarding the relevance of the ombudsman in the American corrections system occurred. In view of our limited experience with correction ombudsmen, and the absence of any experience suggesting that the introduction of an ombudsman into any correctional system will have a salutary effect, one can legitimately question the viability of such an all-encompassing recommendation in 1973.

In fact, we now know that the introduction of an ombudsman into an American correctional facility is not a panacea. Disturbances occurred in Minnesota subsequent to the advent of the state's program, and the Pennsylvania Prison Society ombudsman has been permanently locked out of Holmesburg Prison. But the continued threat of prison upheaval, coupled with the growing recognition that existing internal grievance mechanisms are inadequate, leads enlightened correction administrators to seek new solutions. Against this background the role of the ombudsman in American corrections, however defined, but hopefully with respect for the peculiarities of each correctional setting, undoubtedly will be greatly expanded during the next few years. This paper is an attempt to contribute to that process by detailing the approach used in developing Connecticut's program.

In the fall of 1971, John R. Manson, the Commissioner of Correction, advised the Connecticut Planning Committee on Criminal Administration, the state planning agency under the Law Enforcement Assistance Administration, that one of his priorities for fiscal year 1973 would be the establishment of an ombudsman to serve one or more of Connecticut's correctional institutions. The impetus for this was his expressed concern that the Department of Correction's internal grievance mechanisms were not working satisfactorily. At that early date, Commissioner Manson made it clear that his objective was to establish an office independent of the Department. He believed this was necessary if the ombudsman was to have credibility with inmates and sufficient independence to be able to effect change.

In the summer of 1972, with a commitment of LEAA funding in hand, the Commissioner first approached the Hartford Institute of Criminal and Social Justice, a nonprofit corporation engaged in developing and implementing change in the administration of justice in Hartford, about undertaking the development and operation of the proposed program. He explained that he believed his objective of establishing an ombudsman independent of the Department of Correction would best be achieved if the program was initially developed and operated by a private agency such as the Hartford Institute rather than either the executive or the legislative branch of state government.

In return for its commitment, the Institute requested that Manson commit himself and employees of the Department of Correction to par-

ticipate in a lengthy, intensive development effort, and to guarantee Institute staff access to correctional facilities and personnel. It also requested that the Commissioner agree to have the program operate
initially at no more than three correctional facilities. This latter request was based on the concern that the program would not be successful if the ombudsman was overextended and that more than three
institutions, because of case load size and travel requirements, initially would present an unbearable workload. The Commissioner agreed
to these requests.

During the preliminary discussions, it was recognized that in
order for the program to become an effective grievance-resolving mechanism, two things would have to be achieved during the planning phase:
the concept would have to allow for tailoring the operation of the program to the realities of each participating correctional institution, and
it would have to become operational without causing dissention on the
part of staff and inmates and/or disruption of the day-to-day functioning of the institution.

The desirability of an intensive development phase, designed to
educate Hartford Institute staff about the operation of the Department
of Correction and its facilities, and to fully involve administrative and
institutional personnel of the Department in the development of the program, was recognized. It was agreed that this phase should include, in
addition to frequent meetings between Hartford Institute staff and Department personnel, observation of institutional operations, an exploration of issues with outside experts, and visits to operating programs,
such as the one in Minnesota.

Hartford Institute staff, the Commissioner and members of his
staff, and the wardens of the Hartford Correctional Center and the
Connecticut Correctional Institutions at Enfield and Somers, the three
institutions selected for initial consideration for the program, met in
October 1972. Hartford is a detention and short-term facility, Enfield
a long-term minimum-security facility, and Somers a maximum-
security facility; all house males only.

A number of important decisions were made that set the tone for
program development and began to shape program direction. One issue
that was not resolved was the precise definition of the ombudsman's
role. It was decided that this definition should evolve out of the planning process. A direction along the lines used in Sweden, with an emphasis on change through persuasion rather than by mandate, did begin
to emerge immediately and eventually became the basis for the definition adopted:

> an impartial person, operating within prescribed proce-
> dures and guidelines, for the purpose of resolving inmate
> complaints relating to the functioning of the institutional
> community.

It was recognized at this first planning meeting that in addition to this definition, clear procedural guidelines for the program would have to be developed before it became operational.

The issue of access was resolved at the first meeting. It was recognized that it was necessary to avoid the opportunity for ad hoc decision-making at a time of crisis. The Department agreed that the ombudsman should have twenty-four-hour access, except in the event of a disturbance, in which case his movement inside should be governed by the same restrictions as those imposed on institutional staff; it was agreed that the ombudsman should abide by all institutional rules. This resolution was designed to prevent even a temporary lockout, which, by everyone's agreement, would undermine the program.

Furthermore, it was agreed that institutional and departmental staff would be accessible to the ombudsman for investigation purposes; on his part, the ombudsman would attempt to minimize interference with the performance of assigned duties.

The issue of access to institutional records and the results of Department investigations was discussed. The only resolution was a clarification of positions: the Institute's position that the ombudsman have total access, and the Department's desire to protect the integrity of its records coupled with its concern that state law prohibits the release of certain information (including medical and psychiatric records). This matter was subsequently resolved during the orientation period. All relevant records are available to the ombudsman, limited only by the condition that access to certain records must be requested.

It was agreed that the ombudsman would have access to disciplinary hearings, not as an inmate advocate but as an observer of the general process and the particular situation. Such access eventually was expanded to include all institutional hearings. In addition, the issue of the use of a camera and/or tape recorder by the ombudsman was discussed. The Department's position was that such devices could be used by the ombudsman, but that it was important for the wardens to have advance knowledge in order to give timely notice to subordinate personnel, thus avoiding conflicts between such personnel and the ombudsman arising out of a lack of forewarning and a claim of a violation of institutional rules.

The processing of the ombudsman's recommendations also was discussed. The ombudsman would not, of course, have the authority to order the Commissioner to accept a recommendation. Therefore, in order to maintain the integrity of the program, the ombudsman would need to have the right to press further in the event the Commissioner refused to accept a recommendation. Recourse to either the Governor or the Legislature was not seen as the solution. Recourse to the public, in an attempt to bring pressure on the Commissioner to change his position, appeared to be the most logical solution. It was agreed that a recommendation in a particular case would be made public at the time of the impasse, and process for doing this was delineated.

It was decided that the Hartford Institute would take at least three months to explore the attitudes of employees and inmates regarding the introduction of an ombudsman into the Connecticut correctional system. It would then recruit and hire the ombudsman. The ombudsman would have a two-to-three-month orientation period, meeting and talking with inmates and institutional and Department staff concerning their problems and ideas, before accepting complaints.

The second planning meeting involved only Hartford Institute staff and the wardens of the three institutions under consideration for inclusion in the program. Several critical decisions were made at that session that, in retrospect, were important in defining the ombudsman's role.

For example, it was decided at that meeting to require inmates to exhaust internal institutional grievance procedures before filing a complaint; to treat the failure by the Department to process and resolve such grievances in a timely fashion as the basis for a complaint; and to have complaints resolved informally whenever possible, so as to avoid the more time-consuming process involved in proceeding with a written recommendation. Agreement on this point avoided the possibility that the ombudsman would only become a replacement for existing grievance mechanisms.

The matter of confidentiality of oral and written communications between the ombudsman and inmates was first raised at this second planning meeting. Hartford Institute staff recognized that while the protection of such information would be important in maintaining credibility with the inmates, guidelines would also have to be acceptable to institutional personnel and still be flexible enough to allow the ombudsman to conduct his investigations. The Hartford Institute therefore took the position from the very beginning that while the ombudsman's records would be treated as confidential, the ombudsman would reveal the name of a complainant and the details of the complaint when this was necessary to enable him to conduct an investigation; he would also disclose information about illegal or disruptive acts, such as that relating to physical harm to persons or disruption of the institutions. While most of the issues relating to confidentiality were not resolved until much later, it was agreed at that time that the Department would not censor written communications between the ombudsman and inmates.

Next, separate meetings were held with institutional employees and inmates at Somers, Enfield, and Hartford. No institutional or Department staff attended the meetings with inmates.

The Hartford Institute was concerned about the selection of the inmates for these meetings and would have preferred to have the inmates choose their own representatives. The Department felt this was not practical. Since there were no formal inmate groups or mechanisms to facilitate such a selection, it was decided to let the administration choose the inmates, with the request that those selected represent a cross section of the respective populations. There was a concern that this manner of selection would threaten the credibility of the program among the inmates; it was decided to proceed this way, however, because of a desire to quickly involve inmates and the feeling that any concern on the part of inmates that they were not afforded an adequate opportunity to participate fully in the early development of the program could be overcome during the orientation period, when all inmates would have access to the ombudsman before the finalization of the guidelines of the program. The inmates felt that they did, in fact, reflect a cross section of attitudes, race, nationality, and age within the respective inmate populations; and the fears on this point never materialized.

The meetings with employees revealed significantly differing attitudes from institution to institution. The greatest resistance to the concept was expressed at Somers, the maximum-security facility, and not exclusively from custodial personnel. For example, the medical staff and clergy were openly negative. Overall, the meeting at Somers was useful in that it highlighted points of resistance that would have to be dealt with. Despite the evident hostility, employees began to ask constructive substantive and procedural questions.

The employee session at the minimum-security facility at Enfield provided the Institute with another perspective on employee concern. Generally, the Enfield staff, perhaps because they worked in a less tense and less custodial-oriented environment, was less hostile to the concept. In fact, the head of one of the employee unions at Enfield pointed out the possibility that with the opportunity to participate in its development, the ombudsman program might provide staff with a new opportunity for shaping change in the institution.

The reaction of the staff at the Hartford Correctional Center was enthusiastic. They were anxious to have the program start, and pledged full cooperation to make it a success.

During the meetings with employees at Somers and Enfield, a request was made to Hartford Institute staff to meet alone with the membership of the largest of the employee unions. The Institute declined when the union refused to allow the wardens or their designates to attend. The Institute felt that since the unions had specifically been requested to send representatives to open meetings in the institutions, the wardens or their designates should be invited to attend union meetings open to the rank and file. Recognizing, however, that it was meeting privately with the wardens, the Institute staff agreed to meet alone with the executive board of the union and advised the Department of its intention to do so.

The union was hostile to the proposal. The primary reason for this hostility was the concern that the proposal represented another effort by the administration to mollify inmates. This hostility persisted throughout a lengthy session; and the meeting concluded with the realization that while it was unlikely that the union would seek to block the program, it could not be looked to for more than token acceptance, at least prior to implementation.

The union's major demand was that in cases involving alleged employee misconduct, the ombudsman permit an employee to have union representation during any interviews. The Hartford Institute assured the union that its demands for both union representation and notice to employees before the commencement of an ivestigation would be honored in the final written guidelines of the program.

It became apparent during this session that if the ombudsman was an ex-inmate, he would have a difficult, if not impossible, task in developing credibility with correctional officers. It also appeared unlikely that their hostility toward an ex-inmate in this position could be overcome prior to the commencement of the program.

The reaction of the inmates at the three institutions paralleled staff reactions to a remarkable degree. A wariness toward the program was expressed in all three institutions, most intensely at Somers and least intensely at Hartford. Somers was the only institution where inmates refused to identify themselves to Institute staff and, in at least one case, refused to participate in the discussion. The groups at Somers and Enfield both suggested that inmates should participate with the ombudsman in the operation of the program.

These sessions with inmates produced useful planning information. It was generally agreed by the inmates that race should not be a serious factor in the selection of the ombudsman and that an ex-inmate would have greater credibility with inmates but probably would meet with adverse reactions from custodial personnel. Concern was expressed that the ombudsman should have a private office available to him to meet with inmates and that he should afford inmates complete confidentiality regarding oral and written communications, including not revealing a name if so desired. The inmates took the position that only the complaining inmate should be able to waive the right of confidentiality, with the recognition that an investigation would have to be discounted if the ombudsman felt he could not conduct a thorough investigation without revealing the name.

The inmates appeared to understand the concept being proposed and to perceive the possible benefits for themselves. They expressed hope that an effective ombudsman would improve communications with institutional and Department personnel. They wanted the ombudsman to have access to inmates in segregation and to provide all inmates with copies of the final guidelines and procedures. They, as well as the employees and the union, doubted the ombudsman's ability to cover three institutions and suggested that he service only the number of institutions that he could handle effectively. They were also helpful in that they identified the problem areas with which they felt an ombudsman could deal.

During November, December, and January, the Institute staff continued to meet regularly with the original planning group from the Department, including the Commissioner. A written set of draft guidelines for the program began to evolve. Institute staff prepared the initial draft and all subsequent revisions. Lengthy discussions preceded every change and, where appropriate, compromises were reached between conflicting positions. For example, the position of the warden at Somers that he would have to grant permission for use of a tape recorder was compromised to give him only the right to know when a tape recorder was going to be used.

The Hartford Institute discussed the progress it was making, as well as the draft guidelines, with several outside sources. In addition, a member of the Hartford Institute staff spent two days in Minnesota discussing that program with the Minnesota ombudsman and employees of the Minnesota Department of Correction, including Commissioner David Fogel. Several key issues were considered part of the planning process as the result of these discussions.

For example, Commissioner Fogel offered the opinion that it was unnecessary to engage in a long planning process. His suggestion was to start the program and work out any problems during its operation. This approach was rejected, primarily because of the feeling gained in talking with institutional officials in Minnesota that even though the Minnesota program was operating, they did not fully understand it, appreciate the potential benefits, or have a sense of commitment to it.

Linda Singer of the Center for Correctional Justice in Washington, D.C., recommended that the final agreement be made legally binding on the Department of Correction. She felt that such an agreement would be the only protection against an arbitrary decision by the Department to terminate the program. This recommendation was also rejected because of the feeling that though such a provision could guarantee access for the ombudsman, the negotiations of it would probably create hostility between the Hartford Institute and the Department that might threaten the whole program. The Hartford Institute staff felt that the program would be more successful if the relationship reflected voluntary trust rather than forced cooperation.

The recruitment of an ombudsman began in early March. By then, work with Department personnel, institutional staff, and inmates had produced enough of a mutual understanding regarding the role of the ombudsman and his working relationship to the Department, institutions, and inmates to make it timely for the orientation period to begin. It also was felt that further work on the agreement should await the input of the ombudsman.

The recruitment of an ombudsman turned out to be a difficult task. The first step was to decide on qualifications. Advice was sought from persons of varying backgrounds—inmates and ex-inmates, correctional officers and administrators, and experts working on correctional reform both within and outside Connecticut. It seemed clear that the selection of a person who was either an ex-inmate or an ex-correctional officer or administrator would be received with considerable hostility by the other group. Administration and some correctional staff were hostile to the hiring of an attorney, for fear that he might find it difficult to abandon his traditional role of advocate and might tend to become a generator of lawsuits, thus changing the focus of the program.

Race did not appear to be a critical concern. While some black inmates and ex-inmates expressed the opinion that the substantial black populations in the institutions under consideration might relate better to a black person, they generally agreed that whoever the ombudsman, he would ultimately be judged on his ability to produce positive results for the inmates and, if this was the case, he would have credibility and respect regardless of his race. An ability to communicate with the sizable Spanish-speaking inmate population was deemed important.

It was decided following these discussions, particularly those with a group of ex-inmates working with the Peaceful Movement Committee in Cambridge, Massachusetts, who were experienced in the establishment of inmate grievance reform at Concord Reformatory, that it would be unwise to select either an ex-inmate or an ex-correctional officer or administrator. The risk to the program from the fact that such a person could not be viewed as independent and impartial by all factions in the institutional community seemed too great. A similar conclusion was made regarding the hiring of an attorney, and for the same reason.

Regarding qualifications, an appreciation of the complexities of the job made it clear that the ombudsman would need the maturity to deal impartially and fairly with persons having disparate attitudes, some openly hostile; the ability to conduct impartial and fair investigations, evidencing both a capacity for seeking all relevant information and the resoluteness to pursue a fair solution; a willingness to respect and abide by the rules and regulations relating to the operation of a correctional facility; and a commitment to work within the limits outlined in the agreement between the Department and the Hartford Institute, and any subsequent modifications to that agreement.

Relying principally on word-of-mouth recommendations, the Hartford Institute identified a number of interested applicants. These included persons with no prior correctional experience or an academic familiarity with correctional issues, correctional officers, ex-inmates, attorneys, and clergymen. A review of these applications, followed in some instances by interviews, resulted in the conclusion that none was right for the job and that perhaps the best solution was for the Institute to attempt to recruit from outside Connecticut. At the same time, an interest developed in exploring the possibility of recruiting a successful business executive, ideally one held in high personal regard in the Hartford and/or Connecticut community. Discussions with prominent business executives discouraged this approach, for they indicated that it was unlikely that a successful business executive would be either able or willing to obtain a leave of absence for the two-year commitment that the Institute felt it needed.

Despite a number of feelers requesting assistance in locating an ombudsman, no satisfactory candidate was found. The Hartford Institute staff concluded that rather than hire someone with doubtful qualifications, the selection should be delayed and, if necessary, the Department would have to be advised against going forward with the program. This discouraging situation continued through May. Just when the Hartford Institute began to feel hopeless about finding a candidate, contact was made with Arthur Liman, General Counsel to the New York State Special Commission on Attica. Liman agreed to review the draft agreement between the Department and the Hartford Institute and to meet with Hartford Institute staff regarding both its contents and possible candidates for the ombudsman position.

During a meeting with Liman in New York in early June, which was also attended by Steven Rosenfeld, a Deputy Counsel to the Commission, James Bookwalter, a Senior Investigator with the Commission, was identified as a potential candidate. Both Liman and Rosenfeld recommended him highly and stated that Dean Robert McKay, chairman of the Commission, held the same opinion. They agreed with the Hartford Institute staff's assessment of necessary qualifications and believed that on the basis of the coolness and competence he had displayed in the highly charged atmosphere of the Commission staff, he would be excellent for the job.

Discussions with Bookwalter concerning his work with the Attica Commission revealed that the experience had relevance to the job of ombudsman in two ways: it gave him an appreciation of some of the problems in prisons, and the search for balanced solutions in the staff deliberations had familiarized him with many of the sensitive issues relating to prison life that he would have to face as ombudsman. He appeared to have a good working understanding of how these issues are played out on an everyday basis inside a prison. Consequently, Bookwalter was offered the job, and he accepted it in the middle of June. A concern regarding Bookwalter's selection was the expectation that the inmates would want him to relate his Attica experience to his day-to-day work as ombudsman, and that the institutional staffs would assume

that he had a preconceived commitment to impose the reforms recommended by the Attica Commission on Connecticut. This concern proved
to be unjustified in both cases.

The hiring of Bookwalter moved the program to the final phase
of development, a three-month orientation period for him in the institutions. A decision was made shortly after he started his orientation
that it would be too much for the ombudsman to handle more than two
institutions. Somers and Hartford were selected; Somers because inmate complaints are most frequent and of a greater magnitude there,
and Hartford because of the desire to gain some experience in dealing
with the concerns of pretrial detainees and short-termers, who dominate a correctional center population, in anticipation of expanding the
program to handle the six correctional centers in the state.

During the orientation period, the need to refine program guidelines was identified. Two issues regarding confidentiality were finally
resolved; one major one could not be resolved before the program began. It was decided that the ombudsman should advise a complaining
inmate that anything he learns about a case may be disclosed when it
is "necessary in his judgment to conduct an investigation and support
his recommendations." The complaining inmate must give his "written
permission" to the ombudsman to make such a revelation before an investigation is started. In the event written permission is not granted,
or is subsequently withdrawn in writing, the guidelines provide that the
ombudsman will take no further action on the complaint.

It was also agreed that the obligation of the ombudsman to reveal
certain communications or information, regardless of the source, was
expanded to cover a "criminal act" as well as "a potential danger to
life, or a serious threat to security."

The ombudsman's records are not protected by a statutory grant
of confidentiality. The Department has agreed to treat them as such,
although the courts and legislature are not obligated to do likewise.
Also left uncompleted at the beginning of the program was an agreement
with the Parole Board defining what, if any, role the ombudsman should
have regarding complaints relating to denial of parole.

Despite these and other unresolved issues, the basic objective of
implementing an ombudsman program in selected correctional institutions without inmate and staff rejection or institutional disruption was
achieved with the commencement of the program. Complaints are being
filed, investigations conducted, and recommendations for change made.

Some observations regarding the development of correctional
ombudsman programs can be made on the basis of the Connecticut experience to date. It is unlikely that a program can be properly developed or effectively operated without a commitment to the program by
the head of the Department. This of course requires a willingness on
his part to recognize the existence of problems in correctional institutions, and a commitment to attempt corrective action.

There must be a planning process to resolve issues and introduce the program to interested parties. This should produce written operating guidelines that should be distributed to all interested parties. The planning process should be followed by an orientation period that precedes the acceptance of complaints. The ombudsman should have extensive contact with inmates and correctional officials during the orientation period.

Care should be taken in the selection of the ombudsman. As much time as is necessary should be allowed to make the right selection for each situation, even if it means delaying the implementation of the program.

If these steps are taken, there is no reason why, on the basis of Connecticut's experience, an ombudsman, having the function of Connecticut's, cannot be an effective resolver of specified inmate grievances.

References

National Advisory Commission on Criminal Justice Standards and Goals
    1973   Report of the Task Force on Corrections. Washington, D.C.:
            U.S. Government Printing Office.
President's Commission on Law Enforcement and Administration of
Justice
    1967   The Challenge of Crime in a Free Society. Washington, D.C.:
            U.S. Government Printing Office.

10

THE GANG AND THE COMMUNITY: THE CASE OF THE URBAN LEADERSHIP TRAINING PROGRAM

Although it has long been agreed that program evaluation should consist of more than a simple score-keeping process of recording successes and failures, there are few studies that adequately describe the dynamics of program process or that link research observations to larger social issues. Most evaluations have not considered the social and political context of the experiment and, generally speaking, are written from the perspective of the staff rather than from the viewpoint of the program participant. Moreover, few studies have explicitly recognized that therapies aimed at individual resocialization have important implications for broader strategies of social change. For example, a program that attempts to commit the delinquent to positive and active participation in his immediate community must have implications for other members of that community. We should ask not only what the impact of the program experience was upon participants, but also how their changed social participation would affect the lives of their fellow group members.

This paper analyzes the factors that led to the demise of a program designed to reach hard-core delinquents. Specifically, we will deal with the uses of a delinquency program to the institutions and organizations that planned, supported, and executed such an experiment. Implicit in this analysis is the notion that programs that best serve institutional or political ends often poorly serve the needs of the delinquents who participate in them. The present paper is a reappraisal of research observations reported more fully elsewhere (Krisberg, 1971).

The Urban Leadership Training Program

The chief aim of the program was to train twenty-two young black gang leaders, aged eighteen to twenty-three, to be affirmative community leaders. It was a joint undertaking involving a major Eastern university and a black community organization that functions in an economically depressed neighborhood adjoining the university campus. The program was proposed by the leaders of the community organization to several members of the university staff. Members of the University Management Research Unit helped draft a proposal and persuaded university officials to donate classroom space for the experiment. The director of the Criminology Research Center agreed to supervise the evaluative research on the project. Several other members of the university staff volunteered their services as instructors or technical assistants to the program. Limited funding was provided by a number of small grants from local civic organizations.

The students were leaders of five juvenile gangs in the target area. Each gang leader was a public school dropout. Their combined arrest records totaled more than 175 contacts with the law. Most had served up to thirty-six months in state and local prisons. Their employment histories had been transitory and primarily unsuccessful. Program planners hoped to select students who had demonstrated leadership potential through their gang activities. Staff members of the community organization contacted some of the more influential neighborhood gang leaders and discussed with them the purposes of the Urban Leadership Training Program. The gang leaders recruited members from their own groups to participate in the program.

The training program consisted of a twenty-one-week, full-time course that mixed formal classroom instruction on the university campus with fieldwork in the adjoining community. Courses included economics, sociology, communications, criminology, law, community health, political science, and black studies. Part of the instruction was provided by members of the university faculty and part by staff of the community organization who had been working for some time at solving neighborhood problems. Students received regular salaries of $80 per week during the program. Moreover, the group was to receive a share of the profits from a sixty-minute documentary film made about the entire project. The costs of the filming were provided through a grant from a local firm. The community organization promised to find jobs in community service for each program graduate at the conclusion of the training period.

A central premise of the Urban Leadership Training Program was that the abilities and energies of hard-core delinquents could be redirected into positive and socially desirable projects. The gang delinquent could be "cured" by providing an opportunity for him to benefit his community and thus to be reintegrated with socially meaningful groups. Philip Rieff observes:

> From Plato and Aristotle, through Burke and de Tocqueville, the therapeutic implication of social theory is

remarkably consistent; an individual can exercise his gifts
and powers fully only by participating in the common life.
This is the classical ideal. The healthy man is, in fact,
the good citizen (1966:68).

If the community itself is disordered, then social theories are constructed to reorder social life in ways such that personal salvation can
be obtained through participation in attempts to found a more perfect
social order.

The educational content of the Urban Leadership Training Program was aimed at convincing the delinquent of the desirability and
necessity of his commitment to his fellow neighborhood residents. Further, the specific courses suggested a number of ways in which trainees
could become directly involved in efforts to improve the community.

The Demise of the Program

The Urban Leadership Training Program had style. Its twenty-
two main actors were filmed daily, tape-recorded, and proudly displayed to business leaders, city officials, and U.S. Congressmen. The
gang leaders sported attractive summer jackets that announced their
affiliation with the program, and they carried portable tape recorders
given to them by the research staff to help "facilitate data collection
for the evaluation"—but which were more often used to record the most
popular music of the time. After nearly four months of a reasonably
successful educational program (Krisberg, 1971), the gang leaders and
project staff celebrated their apparent accomplishments with a seven-
day, all-expense-paid trip to Puerto Rico, financed by a major beer
company and by funds made available through the Criminology Research
Center. There was an elaborate prom with over 200 invited guests and
a cap-and-gown graduation ceremony, complete with diplomas.

Ceremonies marking the end of a training program are happy occasions for participants and staff members, but far more important to
the ultimate success of the project are the events that occur after the
formal training sessions have been concluded. The ULTP gang leaders
often expressed the fear that "this would be just another training program," meaning that they would not receive the promised employment
opportunities and would be compelled to return to former activities.
Tragically, their fears were well-founded, despite apparently sincere
efforts to avert the errors of other training programs.

After the close of the training period, trainees worked at their
community projects full-time for approximately six weeks before a fi-
nancial crisis within the community organization limited the amount of

money that they could be paid for their services. Program trainees
were extremely upset with the decline in their income. The program
graduates, who had never really experienced the rewards of community
work (as had regular organization staff), could not accept the cuts in
salary that were more easily borne by permanent staff members. Many
of the ULTP graduates felt betrayed by the community leaders who had
promised, but not obtained, full-time employment for them. Several
gang leaders returned to the illegal activities that had partially supported them prior to their program involvement, and they began to neg-
lect their assigned community projects. Leaders of the community
organization accused the ULTP gang leaders of "hustling on the program," placing full responsibility for the program's apparent failure
upon the trainees. The only remaining source of funds for the gang
leaders was their share of the profits from the film made about the program, but this support seemed extremely uncertain because the docu-
mentary remained unfinished and the film makers reported that it had
little chance of ever making a profit. [1]

To conclude that the ULTP graduates were angry and disillusioned
hardly seems adequate to express the frustration and bitter disappointment experienced by the young men who had completed the program.
Several program participants experienced personal tailspins after the
abrupt end of the program. Two graduates became heavy narcotics
users during that summer. The demise of the program represented a
tragic destruction of the hopes of and for these youthful leaders, who
were too familiar with deprivation and with feelings of failure throughout their lives.

For the community organization, the post-program events meant
a severe, perhaps unrecoupable, setback in plans to enrich the lives
of neighborhood residents. A corps of leaders who would reach the
neighborhood youth engaged in destructive gang violence and who would
provide meaningful resources for the future expansion of community
redevelopment was not the result of the Urban Leadership Training
Program.

In Search of Some Answers

In an attempt to explain why the program "suddenly" collapsed
we observed:

No attempt is made to fix specific blame upon persons
or organizations involved in the U. L. T. program, because
the assignment of guilt is insufficient to account for the
events which followed the U. L. T. program's completion
(Krisberg, 1971:338).

Straining to approximate detached analysis, we searched for general
forces that account for the failing of many well-intentioned experiments.
These forces include the chronic budget problems of community organizations, the difficulties of obtaining continued program funding from
governmental agencies, the insufficient efforts by community leaders
and university personnel to plan for the post-program placement of
graduates, and the failure of the project staff to better prepare the
graduates to face the sacrifices entailed in community service.

But these "answers" remain uncomfortably inadequate. A number
of unresolved questions persist. How was it possible that talented community leaders, experienced project staff members, and skilled university faculty were unable to anticipate and respond to the problems of
providing a meaningful program follow-up? What accounted for the
high level of shared optimism about the program that caused practical
men to fail to grasp the harsh realities of the post-program situation?
Finally, why did community organization leaders place the entire bur-
den of guilt for the program's demise upon the ULTP gang leaders?

To provide a more satisfying and less sociologically naive response to these questions is to state an obvious but often unspoken
observation—that the interests or goals of program participants differ
from the interests or goals of program planners and staff. Institutions
and organizations that sponsor delinquency prevention and resocialization programs receive substantial benefits from such enterprises that
need not be related to successful program outcomes for the delinquents
who participate in them. Indeed, planners, supporters, and staff members accrue many more rewards during a training process and greater
costs at the conclusion of such efforts. While project personnel are
reaping immediate gratifications, the delinquent must defer gratifica-
tion pending possible, but usually uncertain, payoffs at the end of the
training period.

Let us examine the nature of program rewards available to various organizations and individuals supporting the effort. First, we will
consider some payoffs that the university—or, more specifically, some
segments of the university community—received from participation in
the project. Next we examine the positive consequences of the training
program for the community organization. Finally, we explore the rewards that project staff members obtained through their involvement.

The University

The university's involvement in the affairs of the adjoining black
community began approximately three years before the start of the
ULTP. Like many private Eastern schools, the university did not possess a reputation for a high degree of social conscience with respect

to the poor or to minority group members in its immediate environment. Typically, the issue of institutional expansion was central to the first serious confrontation between the academic enclave and the ghetto. A massive University City Science Center, heavily financed by the university, required annexation of substantial portions of land in the adjoining community. Project plans involved redeveloping land that had been used primarily for low-income housing and, thus, displacing many poor families. Initial resistance from the community was present, although not to the degree observed in other localities. [2] In 1968, the year of the college sit-ins, university students seized the administration building and demanded numerous educational and social reforms. Student leaders crystallized their dissent over the issue of the University City Science Center project and the perceived usurpation of the neighboring black community. Peaceful protests resulted in a compromise between students and university administrators that included the formation of a four-party commission composed of students, college administrators, faculty, and community people that would attempt to build a more positive relationship between the school and the community. University plans to complete the Science Center continued without major objections by student or community leaders.

Limited arrangements were begun to include community leaders in some areas to university planning, and some faculty offered their consulting services to an emerging community organization. Most of these efforts were located in the Management Science Unit of the School of Business Administration, apparently with mutually beneficial results (Ackoff, 1970). The university's involvement in the Urban Leadership Training Program was a result of these preliminary collaborative efforts. The program represented the first project in which neighborhood youth were invited to use university facilities to an extensive degree.

Several cues suggested that university officials perceived the project as a high-risk venture. Classroom space was originally planned for two weeks after the project began. A number of university administration staff were assigned to coordinate and to oversee the project. The program participants were forewarned by the project staff that they would be under constant scrutiny by the university community. Their behavior while on campus had to be exemplary, so that opportunities for future programs would not be lost. Throughout the early part of the training, the project coordinator received many reports of alleged ULT trainee misbehavior on campus, reports that attested a fair degree of campus-wide paranoia about the project. Generally speaking, the gang leaders responded admirably to this surveillance, resolving to prove to others that they could be "trusted," although their special status evoked some resentment among them against the university personnel.

Against this background the major reward for the university can be seen. The program represented a symbolic display of the school's sincerity in dealing with the neighboring community. Thus it could be viewed as an attempt to insure peaceful relations with members of that community as well as an attempt to placate university student demands for increased social participation by the school. An additional reward was the public relations benefits that might accrue through publicizing such an effort. Staff of the University Information Service produced numerous press releases celebrating the new program. A brief film about the ULTP was shown during half time of a televised college football game. This same film was given to all local television news shows. There was a story about the project in the student newspaper.

Many of the faculty who participated in the training program discussed plans for future collaboration in health, social service, urban planning, and communications. ULT gang leaders were asked to serve as "consultants" to some ongoing research efforts. Program trainees were asked to reflect attitudes of people in their neighborhood on various issues. University faculty and students could study their responses in the relatively protected environment of the campus and thus not have to venture out into the neighborhood.

The Community Organization

For several years the community organization had met with a good deal of success in its efforts to serve people in the neighborhood. The group, a coalition of former gang members, began work with delinquent youth in the community. Youth work activities expanded into a wide spectrum of planning, educational, and social service programs. The organization now has an annual budget of approximately $500,000 and enjoys a good deal of support from the business and political leaders of the city. (Part of this success might be attributed to the stable relationship that the organization has with the university.) Despite this expansion in community services, the organization's strength remained heavily rooted in its ability to control gang warfare among neighborhood youth. [3] Community leaders recognized that in order to continue to have influence on the street corners, they needed a cadre of younger men who were closer to the gang youths. The graduates of the program were to serve this function of maintaining youth involvement in community projects. Moreover, it seemed clear that other, more militant voices were appealing to the gang constituency. The community organization wanted to counteract these newer messages and solidify their program.

A second political end served by the ULTP was to extend the influence of the community organization to more people in the neighborhood.

Before the program began, the community organization had concentrated its efforts in the eastern portion of the area. The desire to extend
services (and political control) to the western half of the community
was reflected in the composition of the gang youths selected for the
program. Almost two-thirds of the training group were members of
gangs in the western half of the neighborhood. Through the incorpora-
tion of these young men into community projects, the organization could
hope to encourage other residents of the community to participate in
its program.

The program participants served another very important function
for the community leaders. Former gang leaders, whose behavior
could be predicted, were introduced to business and government officials in efforts to obtain new sources of funds for neighborhood projects.
Project staff presented four of five of the "best" trainees to executives,
who seemed to delight in tales of former gang violence and to be willing
to reach out to the people of the ghetto. Members of the ULT group
were key participants in discussions involving business ventures, such
as a community-owned movie theater, an automobile service station,
and a laundry service. Most of these enterprises were too large to be
handled by the gang leaders themselves; and after initial encounters
with money sources, the organization staff continued the negotiation
and planning process. The ULT group soon learned the rhetoric that
would appeal to influential people. They were militant, dedicated, and
believable to the extent necessary to "hustle bread from the bigshots."[4]

Project Staff[5]

Small-scale delinquency prevention programs provide valuable
learning experiences for their usually youthful staff. Dedication and
energy of staff members often compensate for lack of specific training
in the required program skills. In the ULTP the coordinator, many of
the teachers from the community organization, and the researcher
were all new to such endeavors. The ongoing demands of the program
forced staff people to increase their expertise and skills in relevant
areas. While this situation often produces desirable consequences,
the potential benefits are greater for the novice professionals than for
the program participants. The experience gained through program involvement often equips staff members to further their own future plans.

Benefits to the staff of prevention projects often are directly related to labor market demands for expertise in specific areas. Thus
the ULTP added several pertinent items to the professional resumes
of its staff members. The irony of this fact is that the manifest purpose
of a training effort is to improve the "employment prospects" for the

delinquent; but it is often the staff members who benefit more directly in terms of future job security, and this is virtually independent of the program payoffs for the trainees. Nascent careers are often helped by involvement in "sincere but unproductive" programs.

The moral dilemmas are particularly acute for the researcher who may or may not continue his commitment to the people whom he observes and writes about. In the case of the Urban Leadership Training Program, the researcher's participation resulted in a lively topic for a doctoral dissertation and partially helped his successful entry into the academic labor force. How does one relate these enormous personal rewards to the plight of the program participants who returned to a former way of life, tantalized but not delivered the rewards promised by the ULTP?

During the writing of the research report, we considered abandoning the entire enterprise and its potential rewards. It was only after several of the ULT gang leaders suggested that we "tell their side of the story" that we reached the difficult decision to make public, within the limits of personal talents, the nature of the program experience for the gang leaders. Perhaps naively, we believed that this would contribute to sentiment to prevent future exploitation of delinquents by allegedly well-intentioned training efforts. The morality of that decision will remain ambiguous unless we come to grips with the allocation of resources in delinquency research.

Space will not permit a detailed chronology of delinquency prevention programs; but for our purposes we can dismiss the long and unsuccessful (but continuing) history of individually oriented rehabilitation efforts, and instead focus attention upon three programs that were either highly successful or showed potential for success. In each case, funds allocated for the program were suddenly cut off or redirected, the net effect for the participants being no different than for the ULT gang leaders.

The Cincinnati Social Unit Experiment

The idea for the Cincinnati Social Unit Experiment was drafted in 1914-15 by Wilber C. Phillips. [6] The plan developed in connection with Phillips' efforts to develop public information programs for the New York Milk Fund. More generally, Phillips was concerned with improving the health of the poor. The major goal of the Social Unit was "making democracy genuine and efficient—providing a machinery through which people can express their desires easily and continuously, and putting at the disposal of all the people a consensus of expert skill" (Shaffer, 1971:161). This objective would be realized through the estab-

lishment of democratic social units, on a neighborhood basis, focusing
on block development, coordination of expert resources, and a community council (Shaffer, 1971).

Phillips was able to garner a good deal of support for his plan.
By 1916 the National Social Unit Organization had the support of most
of the philanthropic and liberal intellectual-political elite. The supporters included Mrs. Daniel Guggenheim, Mrs. J. Borden Harriman, William Loeb, Jr., Felix Frankfurter, Felix Adler, and Gifford Pinchot.
A number of supporters believed that the Social Unit idea represented
a practical alternative to the class struggle occurring in Europe during
this period. Others hoped to restore the presumably desirable experience of "village life" in urban centers.

Cincinnati was selected because its demographic characteristics
made it a "typical" American city. The city was composed of distinct
districts that made experimentation in one area possible. The Cincinnati Social Unit Organization began on January 1, 1917, in the Mohawk-
Brighton district of the city. Each of thirty-one blocks was organized
into a block council with everyone over the age of eighteen entitled to
participate in its affairs. The block workers were elected to serve on
a citizens' council; they were charged with the responsibility for identifying needs and guaranteeing that program plans would be developed to
meet these needs. Residents belonging to a particular occupational
group who worked or lived in the district were organized into occupational councils, such as the doctors' council, the welfare council, and
the industrial council. Members of the occupational councils would plan
with the block workers to establish service programs for each block.

The first achievement of the Social Unit Experiment was the establishment of a clinic for child care, public health education, and medical care. Many sources report the success of this effort (Shaffer, 1971:
166). Plans were begun to expand activities into welfare and delinquency prevention, but the project suffered a sudden decline.

In March 1919, Mayor Galvin of Cincinnati declared that the Social Unit program was "a dangerous type of socialism." He said, "I
consider it a dangerous institution in our city and but one step away
from Bolshevism. It aims at establishing a government within a government" (emphasis added; Shaffer, 1971:168). Despite a sincere effort by
Phillips and his supporters to defend the program against these charges,
the mayor pressed his crusade. Phillips announced that he would put
the plan to a vote; and on April 10, 1919, the Mohawk-Brighton district voted overwhelmingly to support the Social Unit idea. These election results did little to save the project, because the mayor used his
control of the local political machinery and sufficiently aroused postwar
"Red scare" fears to close the program.

The Chicago Area Project

The Chicago Area Project of the early 1930s is generally considered the progenitor of large-scale, planned, community-based intervention with delinquent youths. It pioneered the use of workers to establish
direct and personal contact with the "unreached" boys, in order to lead
them toward behavior conforming to the norms of society. The program
was conceived by Clifford Shaw and his associates, and owes its theoretical heritage to the research of Shaw and others, reflected in such
works as The Jack-Roller (1930), Brothers in Crime (1936), and Delinquency and Urban Areas (1942). The theoretical perspective of Shaw
and his colleagues located the causes of delinquency in the dynamic life
of the urban community; differential rates of delinquency were directly
related to demographic and socioeconomic conditions of different areas
within a city. The "ecological approach" assumed that delinquency was
symptomatic of social disorganization, and that the specific adjustment
problem of recent immigrants, together with the problems of urban life,
attenuated the impact upon adolescents of such traditional agents of social control as the family, the church, and the community. Delinquency
was viewed as a problem of the modern city, characterized by the break-
down of spontaneous or natural forces of social control. Shaw's theory
held that the rapid rate of social change to which migrants from a rural
background are subjected when they enter the city promotes the child's
alienation from traditional norms of proper behavior. "Where growing
boys are alienated from institutions of their parents and are confronted
with a vital tradition of delinquency among their peers, they engage in
delinquent activity as part of their groping for a place in the only social
groups available to them" (Kobrin, in Johnston et al., 1970:579).
    The Chicago Area Project rested on an optimistic conception of
human nature as essentially improvable. "Delinquency was regarded
as, for the most part, a reversible accident of the person's social experience" (Kobrin, in Johnston et al., 1970:579). The Project employed
several operating assumptions. First, the delinquent is responsive as
a person within the web of relationships of his daily existence. In practice, this meant that the staff expended great effort to mobilize adults
within the neighborhood. The Area Project attempted to foster indigenous local neighborhood leadership that would carry out programs with
delinquent youth. Residents were sensitized to the importance of their
active involvement in solving community problems. Second, the project
staff assumed that people participate only if they have a meaningful role;
therefore, a collective approach that increased the decision-making
function of local residents was employed. This required that the professional staff restrain its natural desires to direct programs. The

approach called for maximum community participation. The last premise of the Chicago Area Project approach was that there is a core of
people in the neighborhoods (especially those with an orientation toward
upward mobility) who can organize and administer local welfare programs, given proper training and guidance. It was felt that the local
worker had more knowledge of local customs, possessed a natural ease
of communication with residents because he was unencumbered by class
barriers, and through his position demonstrated the staff's confidence
in his capacity to accomplish effective work.

The project consisted of a board of directors responsible for raising and distributing funds for research and community programs. Over
several years, twelve community or neighborhood committees were
developed as "independent, self-governing, citizens groups, operating
under their own names and charters" (Sorrentino in Sechrest, 1970:6).
The neighborhood groups were given loans that matched local funds and
were aided by the board in seeking funding. Personnel from the Institute for Juvenile Research at the University of Chicago served as consultants to the local groups.

Most observers, such as Kobrin (1970) and Short (in Shaw and
McKay, 1969), have concluded that the Chicago Area Project succeeded
in fostering local community organizations that were beginning to attack
the problems related to delinquency. But, in 1957, the State Division
of Youth Services took over the thirty-five staff positions of the Area
Project, and it appears that a vibrant and successful social movement
was quickly transformed into "a rather staid, bureaucratic organization
seeking to accomodate itself to the larger social structure, i.e. to
work on behalf of agencies which come into the community rather than
for itself and its members" (Sechrest, 1970:15). The Chicago Area
Project remains a historical example of a community-controlled approach to delinquency that did not really address the larger issues of
poverty, racism, and exploitation but that resulted in strong, autono-
mous groups of citizens working to reduce delinquency in the context
of the localized standards of social integrity.

Mobilization for Youth

The most significant effort to prevent delinquency on a wide scale
was Mobilization for Youth in New York City. The program began in
1962, after five years of planning. It aimed to service a population of
107,000 (approximately one-third black and Puerto Rican) who lived
in some sixty-seven blocks of New York's Lower East Side. The area
unemployment rate was twice that of the city overall and the delinquency
rate was 62.8 per 1,000 in 1960 (Weissman, 1969:19-20).

The theoretical perspective for the project was taken from the work of Richard Cloward and Lloyd Ohlin (1960).

> ". . . a unifying principle of expanding opportunities has worked out as a direct basis for action." This principle was drawn from the concepts outlined by sociologists Richard Cloward and Lloyd Ohlin in their book Delinquency and Opportunity. Drs. Cloward and Ohlin regarded delinquency as the result of the disparity perceived by low-income youths between their legitimate aspirations and the opportunities—social, economic, political, educational—made available to them by society. If the gap between opportunity and aspiration could be bridged, they believed delinquency would be reduced; that would be the agency's goal (Weissman, 1969:19).

Mobilization for Youth involved five areas: work training, education, group work and community organization, services to individuals and families, and training and personnel. But its core became community organization aimed toward "realizing the power resources of the community by creating channels through which consumers of social welfare services can define their problems and goals and negotiate on their own behalf" (Grosser, in Brager and Purcell, 1967:247). Local public and private bureaucracies became the targets of mass protests by agency workers and residents. The strategy of intervention of Mobilization for Youth assumed the necessity of social conflict for alleviation of the causes of delinquency. Shortly after MFY became involved with direct power struggle, city officials charged that the organization was "riot-producing, Communist-oriented, left-wing, and corrupt" (Weissman, 1969:25-28). In the ensuing months the director resigned, funds were limited, and virtually all programs stopped until after the 1964 election. After January 1965, MFY moved away from issues and protests and toward more technical approaches to social programming.

Summary

In all three programs—Cincinnati Social Unit, Chicago Area Project, and Mobilization for Youth—we can observe the common elements of community-controlled action aimed at affecting the underlying causes of delinquency.[7] In each case funds were either cut off or redirected toward more state intervention, and the apparent progress achieved by each program ended. In at least two of the cases, local political leaders aroused fears of Communism to subvert projects that threatened their political power.

The three programs described above were ended by direct political interference, whereas the Urban Leadership Training Program did
not require such an obvious intervention. Indeed, a careful study of the
history of delinquency prevention in the United States would show that
few, if any, granting agencies or universities have sponsored projects
that openly seek to correct unequal wealth, racism, and internal colonization. The recent demise of extra-murally funded projects in ghetto
communities from East Oakland on the West Coast to Bedford Stuyvesant on the East Coast makes very clear the distinction between projects
funded to pacify the "dangerous classes" and those that are abruptly
terminated because they threaten existing political and economic relations.

Programs involving the community, but ultimately controlled by
organizations and persons whose ethnic, class, and cultural backgrounds differ from those of program clients, are often interpreted by
community residents as subtle forms of colonialism, albeit benevolent,
that do not speak to their needs. What is at stake is the creation of a
structure that would allow community people to participate in the political decisions most intimately affecting their lives.

Notes

1. During the course of the program, the staff at the Young Great
Society attempted to help the gang leaders set up small business ventures that might help support them after the program. These ventures
included a movie theater, a gas station, and a coin-operated laundry.
All efforts met with countless difficulties, and little concrete ever materialized.

2. Recall the dispute between Columbia University and the Morn-
ingside Heights community.

3. See Spergel (in Lerman, 1970) on the generality of this problem.

4. This practice is described by Tom Wolfe (1970).

5. By staff we mean the project director, clerical workers, regular instructors from the community organization, and the researcher.

6. For a complete description of the experiment, see Schaffer
(1971).

7. Although each had a different theory of the nature of the underlying causes of delinquency.

References

Ackoff, R.
    1970   A black ghetto's research on a university. Operations Re-
            search 18: 761-71.
Brager, G. A., and F. P. Purcell, eds.
    1967   Community Action Against Poverty. New Haven: College
            and University Press.
Cloward, R., and L. Ohlin
    1960   Delinquency and Opportunity. New York: Praeger.
Kobrin, S.
    1970   The Chicago area project: a 30 year appraisal. In N. John-
            ston et al., The Sociology of Punishment and Correction.
            New York: John Wiley.
Krisberg, B.
    1971   Urban leadership training: an ethnographic study of 22 gang
            leaders. Ph.D. diss. Philadelphia, University of Pennsyl-
            vania.
Lerman, P.
    1970   Delinquency and Social Policy. New York: Praeger.
Mills, C. W.
    1959   The Sociological Imagination. New York: Evergreen.
Rieff, P.
    1966   The Triumph of the Therapeutic. New York: Harper.
Sechrest, D.
    1970   The community approach to juvenile delinquency. Berkeley:
            School of Criminology, University of California. Mimeo.
Shaffer, A.
    1971   The Cincinnati social unit experiment. Social Service Re-
            view 45: 159-71.
Short, J. F.
    1969   "Introduction to the revised edition." Pp. xxv-liv in Clifford
            R. Shaw and Henry D. McKay. Juvenile Delinquency and
            Urban Areas. Chicago: University of Chicago Press.
Weissman, H., ed.
    1969   Community Development in the Mobilization for Youth. New
            York: Association Press.
Wolfe, T.
    1970   Radical Chic and Mau Mauing the Flack Catchers. New York:
            Bantam.

11

AN ATTEMPT TO DECENTRALIZE ADULT CORRECTIONAL SERVICES

Leonard M. Lieberman

Introduction

During 1971 and 1972, the Illinois Department of Corrections attempted to establish four community treatment centers in various regions of the state. These 150-200-resident facilities were intended as experiments in community-focused correctional services for felons, leading toward an eventual decentralization of the penitentiary system for all but the repetitively violent offenders. Planning groups were formed and full funding was allocated for construction, but the project came to a complete halt in early 1973 with the change of administration within the office of the Governor and the Directorship of the Department of Corrections.

The simple explanation is the change in politics. The actual circumstances surrounding the abeyance (if not the termination of the decentralization scheme) may instead indicate a shift in public attitudes that correctional administrators must acknowledge in planning major community corrections projects.

Departmental Planning Prior to Community Involvement

Before offering local communities the opportunity to develop facilities and programs suitable to their unique characteristics and the needs of felony offenders from their regions, the Department of Corrections had to articulate its objectives for its resident population. After considerable discussion by members of the agency's executive staff, it was agreed that the propriety of community-based programming could best

114

be expressed in terms of a lack of opportunities within isolated mega-
prisons that serve a statewide group. These were categorized as lack
of opportunity for self-determination by residents, of training in specific community job skills, and of evaluation of community socialization
of offenders by institutional staff.

Some of these needs may be met by the establishment of an artificial community, as has been created by the Illinois Department of
Corrections at its Vienna Correctional Center, and the District of Columbia Correctional Complex at Lorton, Virginia. These facilities
attempt to evaluate socialization by allowing the residents opportunities
for self-determination in a community-like setting, with central "public
squares," differentiated housing patterns, and a wide diversity of academic and vocational programs on the institutional grounds and at near-
by universities.

The Department planners also reviewed the post-trial criminal
justice process in Illinois, and the societal and judicial intent of sentencing and criminal commitment. Although the Department of Corrections does not have responsibility for probation services in Illinois,
this post-trial component of the criminal justice system was included
in the planning, as were noncriminal commitments and referrals, such
as Department of Mental Health drug-abuse programs. A summation
of the motivations of the courts in sentencing and commitments, and
the alternatives available to meet these judicially determined needs, is
illustrated in Figure 11.1.

For the Adult Division correctional process, the community treatment centers would be under Regional Services. Although the Department envisioned the community treatment centers as being primarily
for short-term offenders not in need of intensive treatment programs
and maximum-security custody, it is feasible that the centers could
also have functioned as a phase of reentry into the community for long-
term or violent offenders who had responded to correctional programming and were ready for limited-contact, community-focused
rehabilitation.

Having a network of community treatment centers allows the Department of Corrections to program its remaining maximum-security
institutions to the few high-security-risk offenders assigned there.
Presently, without community treatment centers, the Department provides security based upon its most dangerous residents while attempting to establish programming that offers the greatest opportunity for
self-determination by the offenders. These objectives are contradictory, and thus Corrections has always had a dichotomy within its institutions between program staff and security personnel. Such conflict
may always be present in correctional facilities; but once it is recognized that rehabilitation efforts (when defined as self-determination;
that is, becoming a responsible, productive member of society) are

FIGURE 11.1

Post–Trial Criminal Justice Process

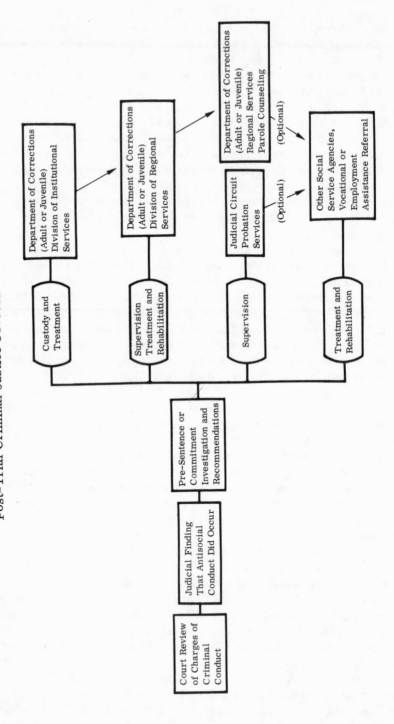

almost futile in a maximum-security, totally structured environment, the allocation of resources for types of programming may be better decided in the context of required security and the rest of the correctional process.

For example, as an offender needs less secure surroundings and is willing to act rationally and constructively, rehabilitative programs should be offered in greater amounts. These programs are offered not as a reward, but as a service for which the inmate, through counseling and self-actualization, is becoming prepared, and from which he will achieve maximum utilization. Programming is expanded, and custody and counseling are diminished, as the offender progresses toward total self-sufficiency in the free community.

Referring again to Figure 11.1, most offenders in need of any residential treatment would be programmed at the community-based center, under the category of Regional Services. Only 20 percent or less of the offenders coming from the courts would be referred to maximum-security facilities, under the heading of Institutional Services, with gradual phasing through Regional Services and Parole Counseling occurring throughout the indeterminate sentencing time frame.

Selection of Regions for Initial Decentralization

The decision to place community-based facilities in the appropriate regions of the state necessitated two investigatory processes: identifying the areas of the state with the greatest present and growing crime rates and felony offenders, and recognizing the communities having the need for a facility that would be the most supportive of a locally focused treatment and socialization program. Once the crime and offender statistics were analyzed (with the assistance of the Illinois Law Enforcement Commission and the Department's own data processing resources), six regions were selected for consideration as sites of the four facilities budgeted by the Department.

A Public Hearing Board was appointed by Director Peter B. Bensinger, under the leadership of former State Criminologist Arthur V. Huffman. Composed of executives of the Department of Corrections, a former director of the Federal Bureau of Prisons, a state legislator, and representatives of the Illinois Chamber of Commerce, the Adult Division Advisory Board, National Council on Crime and Delinquency, the John Howard Association, and other state agencies, it held open sessions in the six communities and regions under final consideration. At each hearing during May-June 1972, it was stressed that the state through the Capital Development Board, would be paying for these facilities with funds already appropriated. Also, the communities selected

would not be asked to contribute toward construction planning costs,
such as local planning sessions or architect's fees.

The Department of Corrections explained at each public hearing
that it could have decided for itself the locations and treatment modal-
ities for these new facilities, but such a determination would not insure
that the local citizens would become involved in the administration and
programming for their local offenders. Also, creating one facility and
treatment model for all four community centers would not be address-
ing the unique program strengths and correctional needs of each region.

Therefore, the Public Hearing Board stated that it had come to
each urban center in recognition of the need for locally based programming in the area, and to seek a commitment from the civic and business
organizations in that region to assist the state in planning a facility appropriate to the community and its unique program strengths and offender profiles.

It was also stressed that the Department of Corrections did not
intend to place a facility that could be considered a "prison." Since the
Department already has four maximum-security correctional com-
plexes, what was being sought were minimum- or medium-security
treatment centers of 150-250 residents that would utilize community
resources as much as possible, would employ local residents as full-
time and part-time workers, and would be responsive to community
interest and involvement. These new facilities would experiment with
innovative approaches to correctional treatment, and only offenders who
were residents of the region and were returning to that community woul
be assigned there.

Based upon the reactions and proposals of local civic leaders,
university representatives, social service organizations, business and
union leaders, and concerned citizens, the Public Hearing Board in
June 1972 selected four regions for initial decentralization—the metro-
politan areas of Chicago, Peoria, East St. Louis, and Rock Island-
Moline.

Organization of the State Planning Task Force

To complement the local planning venture that was about to begin
in the four selected regions, a Department of Corrections Planning
Task Force was created under the chairmanship of Arthur V. Huffman.
Several Public Hearing Board members were joined by representatives
of the State Architect's Office, the National Clearinghouse on Correctional Architecture, the Illinois Law Enforcement Commission, and
Department of Corrections Adult Division treatment executives. This
state-level task force was the link to the Department of Corrections

and other state and federal governmental units the local planners desired to contact, and it has been the Department's only vehicle to lend
support and consultant services to the four communities involved.

When the local communities completed their planning, their facility and rehabilitative proposals would have been subject to the ap-
proval of the state Planning Task Force. To diminish even further the
very slight chance of a rejection of a local planning concept, the Planning Task Force had designated liaisons from itself to each of the regional planning groups, who served as consultants to the local planning
group chairmen.

Other members of the state Planning Task Force served on committees to investigate different facets of facility and program development. Their findings and recommendations were offered to the local
planners as resources, not mandates. These committees had addressed
themselves to physical plant concepts, differential rehabilitation and
treatment programs, and staffing patterns.

Organization of Regional Planning Task Forces

A roster of thirty to thirty-five citizens was compiled from the
recommendations of legislators, local criminal justice officials, and
local civic and business leaders in each selected region. Heading each
local planning group was a chairman or cochairmen appointed by the
state Planning Task Force. In some regions the Department, with the
assistance of the planning chairman, also solicited the involvement of
additional area blacks, women, and ex-offenders on the committee.
All meeting expenses and project-related costs were assumed by the
state Planning Task Force and its fiscal allocation for development
and construction of the new facilities.

Each local planning group had an architect assigned to it, so that
no community-based facility need be related to the other treatment
centers in physical appearance. No formal lines of communication
existed between regional groups, except through the designated regional
liaisons who served on the state Planning Task Force. However, the
various local chairmen were soon in contact with each other to share
organizational experiences. Following the state Planning Task Force
model, each of the regional planning groups appointed subcommittees
to investigate treatment and program concepts, staffing patterns, and
site selection considerations, and to determine the most appropriate
boundaries for their correctional region.

Support of the Department of Corrections in the Planning Process

In addition to making available various members of the Department's executive staff to serve on the state Planning Task Force, various services were extended to the planning process leaders by the Corrections Department.

With the cooperation of the Governor's Office of Planning and Analysis, a survey was conducted of all available, inactive state-owned lands. This report was forwarded to the state Planning Task Force, and shared with local site selection committees. Although local planners were not limited to public lands for facility consideration, each regional site selection committee expressed interest in some of the lands because of their proximity to existing social service agency installations.

The Department of Corrections' Division of Research and Long-Range Planning utilized its Corrections Information System to compile a regional profile of institutionalized offenders, with forty variables on each resident, such as educational level, marital status, vocational skills, security rating, and length of sentence. This regional profile was then made available to the state and regional planning task forces, as a resource for the differential treatment and program planners and the physical plant concept committees. The format of this regional profile was also programmed for all other correctional residents of Illinois, as a resource in determining future development of regional boundaries and facilities.

Other members of the Department's executive staff were requested to address the local planning groups, when invited by the regional task group chairmen, and to arrange visits to existing state facilities by members of the regional groups. To date, comparatively little interaction has occurred between Department staff and the local planning groups. The regional groups accepted the challenge of designing new facilities and programs, and apparently limited benefit was seen in studying the existing institutional correctional process in Illinois.

Concepts Emerging from the Planning Process

Four major planning areas have been recognized by the state and regional task forces, each containing concepts with profound implications for post-institutional corrections development in Illinois and nationwide.

First is the issue of staff profiles. Most planners have agreed that state Civil Service procedures and employee rights present an opportunity for continuation of agency-centered bureaucratization in these new facilities, and give present correctional maximum-security employees first choice of new facility positions without extensive retraining of staff development. A possible solution to this dilemma is that the largest class of facility staff would be program services volunteers, with the next largest being part-time community counseling workers, and the smallest being state custodial and administrative officials. Such a staff compostiton would insure community involvement, would prevent the institutionalization of programming and residential care, and should significantly reduce operating costs.

The second, and perhaps most meaningful, proposal of the state Planning Task Force is the commitment to separating classification and treatment from career opportunity training in location and in program structure. Classification and treatment will consist of diagnosis, setting up rehabilitative strategies and short-term program expectations, and acceptance by the offender of his obligations to himself, to the Parole and Pardon Board (itself perhaps regionalized), and to the community. Rehabilitation and socialization would commence, after treatment had been conducted, in academic and vocational programs throughout the region. Thus, the basic treatment process would occur in a medium- or minimum-security "core" facility to be constructed in each region, utilizing local mental health expertise and area professionals in private practice, and rehabilitation would take place in leased "satellites" near local universities, vocational schools, and industries. Parole counseling could function as an extension of the core facility, a counseling continuum that would provide opportunities for evaluation of offenders and the effectiveness of rehabilitative programming.

Another major emphasis of the planners was upon physical plant, and insuring flexibility. The satellites would be leased by the year, so as to be easily moved or discontinued with changing correctional needs and societal manpower priorities. The core facilities themselves would be constructed modularly, not only for uniformity but also for flexibility on the established grounds, and subsequent possible relocation in the region or dissipation throughout the state.

And last, a difference in direction had appeared between the regional groups with regard to the role of corrections. One local planning group intended to build a criminal justice complex around the state correctional facility, while another group was focusing upon the social service delivery systems in their region. The degree of success of these two contingent models might offer considerable insight into the eventual direction in which corrections must turn, rather than continue to straddle the professional self-concepts of law enforcement and mental health.

Problems Encountered

On the local planning level, few problems were encountered. Some regional groups progressed more rapidly than others, but satisfactory community analysis of criminal justice needs was being done. Since sites were on the lists of available government-owned lands, zoning ordinances were not expected to restrict site selection considerations. For two planning groups, the major locally determined criteria for site selection were proximity to other social service agency installations, universities, professional clinics, and urban transportation systems. And last, the Department of Corrections continued to deal with two areas of controversy centering on the new facilities—charges of offering the regional groups too little direction in the planning process, and resolving the problem of how to limit Civil Service position transfers from the existing maximun-security, institutionally oriented prisons to these new treatment centers without considerable staff development or total retraining. These latter concerns reflected the traditional, agency-oriented view of correctional reform.

The matter of offering direction to the local planners could have been resolved through communications to the public about the total project. Some members of the state Planning Task Force believed that too many recommendations were being offered, such as separating treatment from rehabilitation, extensive utilization of volunteers, and leasing satellites to the constructed core-community treatment center.

The institutional staff transfer dilemma could be resolved in various ways. The few full-time administrative and custodial positions might be initially funded by federal grants, so that new employees could be brought in who would have experience, would not be active in politics, and would be eligible for state Civil Service after one year. Or the Department might draw up entirely new job descriptions for employees of these radically different facilities. A third alternative would be relying upon the newly developing staff training and development program of the Department, which would create a "career ladder," based upon performance, education, and attitude toward offenders, so that employees could transfer to the centers and function effectively.

The major difficulties regarding the development of the Illinois community treatment centers, and therefore the initial decentralization of the state correctional agency, have been the changing public sentiment regarding community-based corrections and the priorities to be set in upgrading the criminal justice system as a whole.

The problem of public acceptance of community-based programming may well be related to the lack of a unified criminal justice system. Communities can hardly be expected to welcome offenders and ex-offenders who are coming to their midst from isolated, deperson-

alized maximum-security facilities. However, the development of locally based correctional centers that are well integrated into the communities will diminish the radical differences in the offenders'
opportunities for self-determination between the penitentiary and the
free society. Thus, the communities' fears regarding the environment
from which the offenders are returning should diminish.

While the Department and the local communities studied the place
of corrections in the continuum of criminal justice planning, the issue
of upgrading probation services received considerable prominence. In
the autumn of 1972, critics of the existing probation system used the
developing correctional community treatment centers as a vehicle for
expounding their viewpoints on their own issue. Although the Department of Corrections did not compete with probation services for LEAA
funding, and corrections is a function of Illinois' executive branch of
government, probation services fall under the administration of local
judicial circuits; various professional associations—the National Council on Crime and Delinquency and the John Howard Association—called
for a national moratorium on the construction of community correctional facilities until the probation issue was resolved. This position was
also articulated by the candidate for Governor of Illinois, who sought
to publicize a difference in philosophy with the incumbent administration while acknowledging the need for a statewide system of leadership
and funding for probation services.

In an earlier attempt to remove the treatment center issue from
politics in an election year, the Department of Corrections and the
state Planning Task Force had purposely delayed the development of
the Chicago area facility. No regional group chairman was designated,
and no roster of members was drawn up.

The Chicago area group never did become formalized, since the
candidate for Governor who campaigned in part against the community
treatment centers and in favor of probation services was elected in November 1972. All other regional groups also halted their efforts, wait-
ing for the new Governor to express his position on the project through
his new director of the Department of Corrections.

A new director was appointed and confirmed by the Illinois Senate
in June 1973. The project was reconfirmed by the Legislature and was
appropriated for in part by the new Governor, but no action in this
area has yet been taken. Hopefully, initial decentralization of state
correctional services for adult offenders will resume, but not without
an almost total reorganization of the local planning units. After almost
a year, many community representatives may no longer be available
to serve, or choose not to participate after so long a breach of support
by the Department.

Hopefully, the planning could resume, restructured to consider
the elements of both probation and institutionalization. A deemphasis

on the "core" facilities, with greater reliance on the "satellites" to
meet periodic imprisonment and probation counseling needs, might be
the way to answer the total correctional process concerns while meeting the greatest social priorities within the criminal justice system.
Under the 1970 Illinois Constitution, Article VII, Section 10, on inter-
governmental cooperation, it is feasible that probation and community-
based corrections could be administered locally, with services
contracted for through the state.

But these new directions still depend upon the public's acceptance
of decentralization as a correctional objective. During the past session
of the Illinois General Assembly, various bills were presented that
would limit the judicial discretion in sentencing offenders to probation.
Most of these bills related to crimes of violence and the use of fire-
arms. Some bills were passed by both houses, and in September 1973
they were signed into law by the Governor. Do those laws represent
a public sentiment away from community corrections? Is the American
citizenry more concerned with humane treatment of offenders within
correctional mega-institutions than with the correctional objective of
reintegration and community involvement?

Conclusion

Decentralization of correctional services in Illinois still appears
to be the proper approach to take. The present prison system has been
acknowledged as a failure by most researchers and by all standards.
Refocusing treatment and programming toward the two major clients
of corrections—the individual offender and the offender's community—
may offer the greatest promise of effective reintegration with maximum
efficiency.

To allow the different regions to develop corrections programs
unique to the urban community is to make available the opportunity to
study and evaluate various types of community-based models. Perhaps
none of these four community treatment centers would significantly
reduce recidivism. But the lessons to be learned from each may substantially add to the knowledge of Illinois Department of Corrections
administrators and other communities, so that the next group of facilities and programs would be a considerable improvement. And because
these first centers might be modularly built with flexibility intended,
the initial decentralization process could be updated with minimal expense or inconvenience.

But correctional administrators must act quickly, for the interest
in corrections is changing. The gains of the last decade must be con-
solidated, and lasting alternatives to mass institutionalization must be

developed. If states continue to move only in the direction of the Massachusetts Youth Services Administration, when the public climate changes to a more conservative posture the states will have only their antiquated institutions left.

Decentralization can succeed in the 1970s; but it calls for phases of community entry, with community centers as one step forward. An extensive public education campaign, to make the public aware of correctional goals and objectives, is another essential step. To move from mega-institutionalization to probation and minimum-security release centers may be too much for the communities to accept today.

Eventually, the Department of Corrections may have only one maximum-security institution serving a statewide population, with all other offenders treated regionally, in community centers and in extended probation programs and facilities. Hopefully, these centers and programs will truly be post-institutional, and the "problem of prisons" will never be repeated. Corrections will continue to evolve only with community interest and direct involvement, and corrections administrators need only maintain that community rapport. If decentralization succeeds, it is the communities' success.

CUSHIONING
FUTURE SHOCK
IN CORRECTIONS

Milton Luger and
Joseph S. Lobenthal, Jr.

Introduction

"Community-based" programming, a current cry in corrections, stems from the idea that offenders must learn to cope with and adjust to the real world, not the artificial milieu of an isolated institution. The criminal justice system alone cannot control the antisocial and illegal activities of acting-out individuals who will pass through the "correctional" phase of their lives and then return, without benefit of intervening community concern, to settings and consequences filled with multiple deficits, such as irrelevant education, slum housing, and racial and job discrimination. These affect many who end up before the courts and in public institutions.

But total reliance upon community-based programming is naive. It leaves administrators with one alternative rather than a well-orchestrated, diversified set of services. Some offenders have demonstrated enough volatile and uncontrollable behavior to indicate that removal from the community is required.

There will, of course, come a time when enthusiasts for community-based programs will temper their enthusiasm with reality. This is likely to occur when the necessity for overselling is a thing of the past. Appropriate community programs can then coexist peacefully with upgraded institutional operations. As this occurs, there will eventually be a reciprocal gathering into the fold of some of the skeptics, so that programs that now seem far-out and radical can be viewed in a calmer perspective as offering beleaguered administrators options that are both natural and helpful.

─────────

This article appeared in <u>Federal Probation</u>, June 1974.

This essay points out that many community-oriented programs that we in corrections are now advocating will, to the extent that they are achieved, trigger special situations and create new problems. The consequences of these programs will, in turn, feed back into the reformed correctional system. The authors suggest that the appropriate time to consider these consequences is now, and that responsive means of action can be developed if professionals will now debate the issues and take a long-range and full-dimensional view of their own proposals.

Some issues pertinent to community-based programs are therefore explored even though they now seem in the Buck Rogers category. Although apparently not of immediate concern, they ought to receive our present consideration. If we do not examine them now, circumstances may make it improbable that we can have an impact upon their resolution at some later time.

The present discussion also seeks to illustrate how the potential and capabilities of community-based corrections are not limited to the functioning of the criminal justice system, but are tied directly to conditions in other aspects of society. Yet, for the most part, our comments about community participation continue to be based on the present and to assume certain constants for the future. Some of these assumed constants are the nature of an institution, the population from which selection of inmates for community activities will be made, the quality of components of the system other than corrections, and the tolerance and receptivity levels of "the community."

It is impossible to pinpoint all of the changes that will occur within the next decade. Nevertheless, A. Toffler (1970) and others have convincingly demonstrated an increasing rate of social change, and we should at least attempt to identify some areas in which change will probably have a major impact on correctional efforts proposed to be practiced outside institutions. This article suggests that certain issues, presently discoverable and debatable, should be dealt with now, even though— or perhaps because—many of their ramifications have to do with the future.

Implementation of Standards Throughout the Criminal Justice System

If some or most of the standards recommended in works such as the report of the National Advisory Commission on Criminal Justice Standards and Goals (1973) are implemented, criminal law administration will be generally upgraded. As a result of effective preventive programs and the exercise of pre-adjudicatory, pre-trial, and pre-sentence options, major diversion of persons from prisons should occur.

Penologists frequently say that a majority of imprisoned inmates require less custody than is imposed upon them in today's institutions. This, however, might not always hold true. If diversionary techniques prove effective, fewer persons than are now in prison—or a smaller proportion of the general population—will be institutionalized. At the same time, sentenced inmates in these institutions presumably will be more dangerous than inmates are at present. The potential universe of those available for community-based programs will, therefore, consist of those who have progressed through a different criminalizing process than exists today.

If, as the result of a hypothetically improved judicial administration, released persons posed grave dangers to society as a result of their negative experience in prison, that fact would have implications for all aspects of corrections. One likely effect would be the questionable potential of present community approaches for these people. Another would be the community's lessened willingness to participate in or tolerate certain kinds of activity. A third would be an increased urgency, from the viewpoint of society, for the development of programs effectively linking the institution and the community.

Perhaps these linking activities will most often take place in the correctional institution rather than in the community itself. Increased use of volunteers in maximum-security settings, more family and conjugal interrelationships, and accredited college work are approaches that have hardly been tapped. But it is also possible that proportionately massive and more concentrated community resources, refined through present experiences and research, and applied with these fewer participants, could dramatically demonstrate the full potential of community-focused interaction.

Social-Control Technology

Future technological development has many ramifications for community corrections that depend on decisions about the correctional use to which new products should and will be put. Technology affects training, employment, the work ethos, the nature of crime, and other factors that are pertinent to the kinds of programs that can be mounted, either in the community or in the institution.

We shall focus here on but one aspect of technology: that specifically applied to social control of convicted persons. Presently existing technological capabilities, whether yet developed or applied in this field, seem likely to have a radical effect on the potential of community corrections. Electronic surveillance devices and biological and chemical controls exist, or are presently feasible and can be produced; use of these devices awaits legal and moral decisions about whether they should be used, how, and on whom.

For example, currently available sensory implants permit contemporaneous monitoring and surveillance of those in the community. There are electronic devices by means of which releasees could report to local transmission stations instead of to a caseworker or to someone within the prison. Many other monitoring inventions that are equally effective mechanically can be adapted for correctional applications. The potential of these approaches might increase the number of inmates who could be allowed to function in the community. Yet, without advocating such use, it is interesting to note the ideological horror expressed by liberal, casework-oriented workers when these issues are raised. The possible modification of a counseling relationship, supposedly based upon mutual trust and support, with an approach that is less subject to manipulation and human frailties seems to pose a threat to many. Yet these very workers offer few alternatives to a swift return to the Bastille when their preferred method has failed.

Tranquilizing or other behavior-modifying pharmaceuticals are also potentially relevant to decisions about eligibility for and participation in community-based programs. For example, emerging biomedical research in drug antagonists might affect decisions about what degree of risk is incurred when an inmate, who would otherwise be vulnerable to drug abuse, is considered for release into the community—assuming, of course, the continued illegality and relative scarcity of narcotics.

At least one court test concerning psychosurgery is currently in the appeals stage; some of the implications of this technique, as well as of sterilization and genetic alterations, are truly staggering.

Unfortunately, those who are most prolific in their treatment of community correction are reluctant to become involved in discussions about issues raised by such developments. Yet there is an unavoidable connection between the two, and at least preliminary consideration of positions ought to be generated within the correctional field.

The authors' position is that devices that presently seem Orwellian should not be rejected out of hand, planned for, or allowed to slip into general use in corrections until the subject has been fully debated in light of such factors as the individual's right to privacy; the implications of centralized state control over the individual; the lack of scientific knowledge about total, long-lasting, or side effects on the human body and personality; the possibilities of such interventions' being abused in practice or as a matter of government policy; and the difficulties of monitoring their use and of controlling abuse.

Part of any deliberation on the subject should be the caveat that no device or technique ever be used without the free and informed consent of the subject inmate. This is important because minors and those with diminished or impaired capacity may be involved, and also because the choice will be a function of whatever institutional and community alternatives face an inmate. If, for example, institutional environments are so horrendous as to create a temporary distortion in or undue pressure on the inmate's decisions, there may be no redress possible for that inmate once a device or drug has been placed in use or a surgical technique employed. The issue of whether it is possible for any inmate, or perhaps any convicted person, legally to give "voluntary and informed consent" about matters of such import is, in the authors' opinion, still to be resolved and a likely subject for judicial determination in the future.

Principles governing the permissible application of this kind of social, control mechanism should be explored. One of the factors to be weighed should be an awareness that its responsible use would rid administrators and the public of realistic fears about placing certain individuals in the community and that this would perhaps diminish the number held in prisons.

Changes in the Power Structure of the Community

Such current movements as that toward community control and decentralization of institutions and governmental instruments can be expected to have an impact on future programs that stress community-institution interaction.

On local urban school boards, community planning boards, and hospital advisory groups, those directly involved in receiving services are taking increasingly assertive roles in setting policy, determining standards, ruling on what services are to be provided, and in overseeing their daily administration. Closer to the matter of placing offenders in the community, citizen forces have become involved in community treatment of the mentally disturbed, including some persons hitherto diagnosed as untreatable.

Simultaneously, pressures have developed and will continue, from within the institution, for greater representation of inmates at all levels of decision-making. Through intervention of prisoners'-rights lawyers and ombudsmen, inmate voices will increasingly be heard at the planning and administrative levels of any program having as its core even the temporary placement of incarcerated persons in the community.

These client-centered movements toward treatment in the community, with the major institution and traditional professional staff functioning primarily as a springboard, are likely to serve as a model for future bridging programs for inmates who are mandated by sentence to be institutionalized but who are allowed to participate in some kind of community program. The community can be expected to assume more direct responsibility for providing services for inmates, thereby automatically creating linking opportunities that cannot be implemented at the current level of community involvement.

It seems likely that inner-city medical and mental-health institutions will be increasingly governed by lay boards to whom staff will be responsible as much as, or more than, to professional supervisors. A predictable result will be that controlling community elements will more closely parallel the cultural and ethnic makeup of clients, since those most personally involved will likely be the most active on these levels on a day-to-day basis. It is inevitable that similar situations will apply in prison institutions.

Pressure may be put on staff to review conventional means of determining eligibility for programs and to offer increased access to those previously perceived as unmotivated or untreatable, especially the poor and minority-group offenders.

Such shifts can be expected to result in marked changes in institutional management through consequent changes in the makeup of correctional staff. Custodial officials will probably come to reflect those held in prison. This may occur as a result of many forces, such as the demands of concerned and representative community groups; diversification of prison services, requiring new kinds of staff; increased access to positions for those who do not rise through the ranks via traditional Civil Service examinations; the development of inmate power, resulting in, among other things, increased use of indigenous inmate and former-inmate paraprofessionals; the development of new professions in correction; and increased mobility and communication between institution and community.

Expanding Definitions of Inmates' Rights

Expanded definitions of inmates' rights will probably emerge from the courts. If, for example, a "right" to treatment is judicially proclaimed and participation in a meaningful program becomes a requisite for incarceration, community correction programs might not be able to be maintained primarily for the benefit of the most amenable, most promising, best-qualified, middle-class inmates. Either significant prison or community-based programs will have to be developed for hard-core inmates or, ironically, these same inmates will be the first released into the community because it will be illegal for them to remain incarcerated while uninvolved and unreached. Society will then be confronted with a choice between absorbing rather than isolating offenders or providing appropriate and adequate community resources to and within the institution.

Another area in which court decisions will be influential in determining the form and scope of future linking activities is that of inmates' rights to organize, join unions and participate in union activities (including strikes, job actions, slowdowns, and the negotiation of contracts), or to receive union wages for their work (whether within or outside the institution). For nonunion inmates, court decisions will be influential in determining the payment of minimum hourly wages as determined by the governmental jurisdiction in which the prison is located or where their labors are performed.

Many administrators view the notion of minimum wages for offenders with ambivalence, fearing that the increased agency budgets that might be required would displease legislators. At the same time these administrators ignore the fact that much of the supposed increase would be offset by charging inmates realistic costs for their maintenance. This does not mean a tradeoff with no net gains for meaningful corrections; rather, in terms of the community's image of the inmate, the inmate's self-image, and the relationship between inmate and correctional system, considerable gains would result.

Even so, it is sanguine and perhaps a little irresponsible to rely overly on the "economy"—or even the "break-even"—argument in support of community corrections. The level of economic analysis that has been applied in reaching the conclusion that community corrections is inevitably cheaper than institutionalization does not seem sophisticated enough to account for new costs that must arise in adapting programs to some of the likely future changes that have been suggested. To urge the concept on economic grounds alone, or primarily on that basis—without emphasizing the reality that economic as well as personal commitment is required in order for significant changes to be made—is misleading and may be, in the long run, a contraindicated strategy for proponents.

A related consideration involves the inmate entrepreneur. Does the aspiring or accomplished inmate artist, jeweler, engineer, businessman, writer, or even politician have the right to ply his trade, sell his wares, or try his hand on the outside in the same way that would be open to those with contracted employment? This question has not been specifically decided. But existing court decisions pertaining to issues such as the inmate's right to publish commercially, and decided on the principles of law such as free speech and access to the courts (for instance, money to discharge Legal Aid and retain private counsel), suggest that the answer is likely to be in the affirmative.

Changing Educational and Employment Patterns

Converging with the effects of institutional changes that have been suggested, the action of forces external to correction will have certain impact on community-based programs. For example, the trend away from formal entrance requirements for colleges and professional schools and the substitution of life-experience credits in their stead, combined with open-enrollment programs for local residents, may result in a tremendous expansion of prison study as the core activity in bridging programs.

Inmates acquiring new skills as a result of prison-academic partnerships will create a need for different post-release placement efforts or, alternatively, perhaps diminish that need considerably. Other ramifications include possible fieldwork placements for inmates within the prison—as interns in agencies, organizations, business, or governmental bodies within the community, in prison hospitals, or in counseling, clinic, or Legal Aid units.

Conclusion

The foregoing are specific examples of how the nature and extent of community corrections depend on, or are interrelated with, factors that often are considered temporally remote from or extrinsic to the proper concern of correctional planners. The implication of programmatic changes should be explored with full awareness of the fact that the once-distant future seems to arrive overnight and issues for the near-term future are latent in the present.

It would be possible to set forth further examples in an essay of greater length. The authors would then especially refer to the potential impact on community corrections of such movements as women's liberation and the sexual revolution as illustrative of present reformist and egalitarian thrusts that should be considered.

The impingement of any important social current on a correctional system that is emerging from isolation and is both being impelled and impelling itself closer to the community is to be anticipated as an influence on operational changes.

References

National Advisory Commission on Criminal Justice Standards and Goals Report.
    1973   Washington, D.C.: U.S. Governmental Printing Office.
Toffler, A.
    1970   Future Shock. New York: Random House.

13

**DOING JUSTICE TO
CRIMINOLOGY: REFLECTIONS
ON THE IMPLICATIONS FOR
CRIMINOLOGY OF RECENT
DEVELOPMENTS IN THE
PHILOSOPHY OF JUSTICE**

Jeffrey H. Reiman

My purpose in this paper is to argue that some recent developments in moral and political philosophy are of extreme significance for students of criminology. The recent developments I have in mind are the articles, debate, and discussion leading to and culminating in John Rawls's A Theory of Justice (1971). Stuart Hampshire, the noted British philosopher, has characterized this book as the most significant contribution to moral and political philosophy in the English language since World War II. My own view is that, if anything, this is too modest. Rawls's work may be the most important philosophical event of this century. It has, in my estimation, taken a giant step beyond the serviceable but strangely unsatisfying doctrine of utilitarianism, which has been the major resource against ethical relativism for the past hundred years. That is, Rawls has offered a solution to the problem of justice that is not only more plausible than that of the utilitarians, but also one that is so powerfully argued as to represent a convincing refutation of ethical relativism.

On the basis of Rawls's work, I am persuaded that the possibility is at hand for intelligently asking and objectively answering the question What is justice? In what follows, I will try first to indicate the outlines of Rawls's method and arguments. Then I will try to demonstrate their significance by tracing out their implications for some recent, important examples of criminological theorizing. Obviously the limitations of time and space are such that my presentation will necessarily be sketchy and suggestive instead of complete and conclusive. However, in a time of increasing specialization and difficulty of communicating across disciplinary boundaries, I shall be satisfied if I have managed to plant the suggestion that something has happened in philosophy that should be noted by criminologists.

Rawls and Justice

Rawls's approach starts from the heuristic assumption that the moral point of view is reasonable: The process of subjecting actions and institutions to evaluation in terms of principles exists and persists in societies because it is in some sense reasonable for societies to devote their energies to this process. The task of the moral philosopher does not end with this assumption; it begins there. He must formulate the theoretical framework in terms of which the varied and sometimes conflicting phenomena of morality (moral rules, moral judgments, moral sentiments) are rendered consistent and reasonable. In this sense the moral philosopher is in a position analogous to that of a social scientist. The scientist and the philosopher are confronted with a mass of varied and apparently conflicting phenomena. Both must begin with the heuristic assumption that these phenomena can be seen to be reasonable; that is, they can be set in an internally coherent theoretical framework, yet are consistent with the rest of the things we know about human beings.

It would seem that the moral philosopher's task begins to get sticky, however, as soon as it is seen that the moral phenomena to be explained include such notoriously intractable concepts as "good" and "bad" and "should" and "ought." But are these really so opaque? A hundred times a day we use these terms without the slightest question about their meanings. If I tell my friend that he should wear a raincoat because it is about to rain, he understands me immediately. I am telling him that, given my knowledge of the meteorological conditions outside (the likelihood of rain) and of his purpose (the desire to stay dry), he will receive something that he will regard as a benefit (staying dry) if he complies with my advice. Now there are many ways in which my advice would be wrong. I might have mistaken a passing cloud for an impending storm. I might have wrongly assumed that my friend wanted to stay dry (after all, some people might enjoy a good drenching). However, these are empirical matters and easily verified. And, if my empirical assumptions prove correct—if it is about to rain and my friend doesn't want to get wet—then my advice to him is both reasonable and true. That is, if statements are ever reasonable and true, then it is reasonable and true that my friend should wear his raincoat.

A similar analysis can be offered for terms like "good." If I tell you that the Hilton is a good hotel, then you know that I mean it scores relatively high in fulfilling the demands of people who use hotels—or, equivalently, it offers a relatively high proportion of the kinds of benefits that one expects from hotels: comfort, service, cleanliness, convenience. If you have some exotic purpose for going to a hotel, then the Hilton may not be a good hotel for you. But this is as much a fact as it is a fact that the Hilton is a good hotel for people with more ordinary designs.

In other words, statements of the form "Person A should do act X" or "Y is good for person B" are quite capable of being tested for their truth and reasonableness. The statements are true and represent reasonable advice, if in fact act X will lead to the fulfillment of some interest or purpose of A's (without, of course, interfering with some other interest or purpose on which he places priority), and if in fact Y confers some benefit, some satisfaction, feeling of worth, or whatever on B (without causing significant losses). Merely to say "Y is good," without specifying that it is good for B, is to state that Y has the capacity to fulfill the interests of, or confer benefits on, all or most people. And all of this can be subjected to empirical testing.

How, then, do we make moral rules reasonable? Can we simply say that the statement "You should tell the truth" is of the same sort as "You should wear your raincoat"? To make this simple identification would be a mistake. The statement "You should wear your raincoat" is true only as long as it fulfills your purpose or is in your interest. But to say that the statement "You should tell the truth" is true only as long as it is in your interest is to take from the statement precisely what makes it a moral statement. Obviously, when we cite a moral obligation to tell the truth, its significance lies precisely in the demand that one tell the truth even when it is not in one's interest. Thus moral rules cannot be reasonable in quite the same way as bits of advice given to individuals.

How can the claim that moral rules are reasonable be upheld? To answer this we must recall that moral rules are a social institution. They are, crudely speaking, taught to all of us by all of us. It is this social dimension that renders moral rules unique. Even though telling the truth and the like may run counter to an individual's interest or purposes, it is relatively easy to see that from the standpoint of society, everyone's interest is better served in a world where people generally tell the truth, even when inconvenient, than in a world in which truthfulness never extends beyond each person's determination of whether it serves his own aims. If anyone doubts this, he should think not only of the value to him of being able to trust others, but of the value to him of being able to talk and make promises to others, and be trusted by them. In other words—and necessarily oversimplifying—such moral rules are reasonable socially, even though they may be unreasonable in terms of a given individual's aims. This is the key to the reasonableness of moral rules—they enshrine the wisdom that everyone's interests are better served when everyone acts by some principles that occasionally restrict his pursuit of his own interests. Thus moral rules are true and reasonable when they are rules that everyone is better off having than not having. Moral rules are true if they are—of all possible alternative rules—those that are most clearly in everyone's interest.

Now what is true of all moral rules is equally true of the segment of moral rules that falls in the province of justice. These are the moral rules that are used to evaluate the fundamental institutions of a society, its legal institutions and its economic institutions. Justice is important because it is the moral evaluation of the ways in which the fundamental things men seek—freedom and wealth—are divided.

How, then, do we ask the question of justice? How do we ask whether the rules defining the distribution of freedom and wealth in society are just? Truly and reasonably just? Can we simply ask whether these are the rules with which everyone is better off with than without them? Even if we could ask this, how would we answer it? How would people judge whether they are better off with the rules than without them? Is a convicted murderer better off with laws against murder than without them? Is the slave master better off with slave labor laws or without them? These questions become obstacles because they reflect the difficulty of raising the question of justice to individuals who are already occupying positions in a system that itself may be just or unjust.

Thus, even if we are correct in our preliminary formulation of the reasonable standard of justice, how can we apply it in society to individuals who already occupy positions and have interests to defend— all of which may be the result of prior injustice?

It is precisely here that Rawls's method proves its fruitfulness. Rawls asks us to imagine a group of rational and self-interested persons who must come to some unanimous agreement on the fundamental principles that will guide their interactions in the future. Since this is an imaginary situation, we can construct it to fit our needs as moral philosophers. Rawls therefore adds what he calls the "veil of ignorance." This stipulates that the individuals in this imaginary original position are ignorant of all the particular features of their own existence. They don't know how smart or stupid they are, they don't know their sex or race or social position. In other words, all the factors that might lead people to place their personal interests over those of others, all the factors that might openly or surreptitiously carry with them the results of prior injustices, are removed from the hypothetical situation. This imaginary original position is constructed so as to be free of anything that might be tainted by injustice: social position, racial or sexual prejudice, and so on. In this imaginary condition we ask for the rules to which it would be rational for all individuals to agree, in order to regulate the limits of their freedom vis-a-vis one another and the distribution of wealth.

Before asking what rules persons so situated would agree to, let's be clear on why whatever rules they would agree to are the true and reasonable rules of justice. First, the rules clearly concern justice— that is, they are rules for the distribution of freedom, wealth, and so on. Second, they are rules to resolve a problem that is constructed to typify problems of justice—that is, the persons who must agree are not selfless saints. They are self-interested individuals pressing claims on one another. Since they are rational, they will settle on rules that are reasonable. However—and this third point is the key to Rawls's argument—because of the "veil of ignorance" they must select rules that are reasonable but do not favor any one person's characteristics over those of another, do not impose any one person's interests on another's. Via the "veil of ignorance," what is individually reasonable becomes what is socially reasonable—what is in everyone's interest. What is reasonable for an individual when he does not know his personal characteristics and social position is necessarily what will be optimally reasonable for him, whatever kind of personality or position he has. Because of the "veil of ignorance" no one can make a special exception for himself, no one knows what his specific interest will be.

In sum, the principles that would be agreed upon in the imaginary original position behind the veil of ignorance are the true principles of justice, because they are the reasonable rules by which men can guide themselves, when the conditions under which it would be reasonable to promote unjust rules are eliminated. They are the principles of justice because they are proper moral rules applied to the fundamental legal and economic institutions of society. They are the rules under which these institutions would optimize everyone's interest.

Rawls goes on to argue that individuals so situated would agree to the following two rules as overriding principles:

First Principle
Each person is to have an equal right to the most extensive total system of equal basic liberties compatible with a similar system of liberty for all.

Second Principle
Social and economic inequalities are to be arranged so that they are both
    (a) to the greatest benefit of the least advantaged . . ., and
    (b) attached to offices and positions open to all under conditions of fair equality of opportunity (Rawls, 1971:302).

I hope it is at least plausible that these principles would be agreed to under the stipulated conditions. Rawls's argument is extremely complex, covering some 600 pages, and I could hardly do justice to it here. More important for my purposes is recognition of the soundness of Rawls's method. That is, the notion that the principles agreed to unanimously by rational, self-interested persons ignorant of their personal interests would be in everyone's interest: the true principles of justice. If this much is accepted, it remains to ask a further question: What is the significance to criminology of the establishment of an objectively valid standard of justice?

Criminology and Justice

I shall deal with this question in the following way. First, I will select two theoretical works on criminology and suggest what the implications for these theories would be if we are persuaded that Rawls has successfully offered an objective standard of justice. Next I will sketch out some of the broader implications of this for the entire enterprise of criminology.

The two works I have selected are Richard Quinney's The Social Reality of Crime (1970) and Richard Cloward and Lloyd Ohlin's Delinquency and Opportunity (1960). I have suggested these two because they take widely disparate approaches, and I assume my audience is familiar with them. Thus, if I can show that the existence of an objective standard of justice has fateful implications for these works, I think I can plant the general suspicion that it has fateful implications for all criminological theory.

I turn first to Quinney's work. Quinney argues that crime is a definition of behavior that is applied by those with the power to design and enforce such definitions. This in itself is neither controversial nor terribly interesting; it merely says that crime is a humanly constructed and applied category, and it is constructed and applied by those able to do so. This statement is practically a tautology. It boils down to saying that law is made by those with the ability to make the law—it could hardly be otherwise. It becomes interesting when a further point is added: the notion that individuals with power tailor the definition of crime to their own interests. Quinney makes this very assertion:

> Law is a form of public policy that regulates the behavior and activities of all members of a society. It is formulated and administered by those segments of society which are able to incorporate their interests into the creation and interpretation of public policy. Rather than representing the institutional concerns of all segments of society, law secures the interests of particular segments, supporting one point of view at the expense of others (Quinney, 1970:40).

The last sentence is the keystone of Quinney's argument. It is obviously a claim that the law is not objectively just. It is not in every-

one's interest. But how can this claim be established? How do we prove
that law (meaning primarily criminal law) expresses particular interests at the expense of the whole of society? One simple but misleading
strategy would be the following. Laws are made by human beings. Human beings act in their self-interest. Ergo laws express the particular
self-interests of lawmakers. But this really tells us very little. It may
still be the case that the particular self-interests of lawmakers coin-
cide (perhaps accidentally) with everyone's particular interests. To
deny that they do is to put us back at square one, still in need of proof
that the laws express particular interests at the expense of other interests.

We could go about this in another way. We could try to identify
the interests actually served by the criminal laws and then compare
these with the interests of everyone in society. If there is a conflict,
then it would seem that Quinney's point is made.

But here too the issue is more complex. What are the interests
of everyone in society? Are they simply those things that people believe
to be in their interest? Or are there some things that are objectively
in everyone's interest whether or not they know it? It is precisely at
this point that the existence of an objective standard of justice becomes
fateful for Quinney's theory. If there is no objective standard of justice,
then what is in everyone's interest is probably no more than the sum
of what everyone defines as in his interest. On this alternative it would
probably be easy for Quinney to prove this point. But if there is an objective (true and reasonable) standard of justice, it represents precisely those shared rules that are in everyone's interest, over and
above their private interests or beliefs about them. If this is the case,
then Quinney has a much more complex task. He must show not merely
that there are some people who do not believe that their interests are
expressed in the law, but that regardless of who makes the law, it does
in fact diverge from what is objectively in everyone's interest (from
what is objectively just). That is, using Rawls's terminology, he must
show that the law diverges from what rational individuals would unanimously agree to when they could not favor their particular interests.
Put conversely, even if the law is made by one selfish and obtuse ty-
rant over the wishes of all his subjects, it still might express their
real interests. If this were the case, then Quinney's claim would be
refuted.

In sum, Quinney's position can stand only if we deny an objective
standard of justice true and reasonable for everyone, and show the di-
vergence of the interests expressed in the law from those expressed
elsewhere in society. If, however, there is a true and reasonable
standard of justice, then Quinney's claim stands only if he can show not
merely that law is made by self-interested individuals, but also that
they make it in such a way as to cause it to diverge from the standard
of justice.

Let us turn now to the work of Cloward and Ohlin. They, like
other investigators of juvenile delinquency, such as David Matza (1964),
emphasize the delinquent's sense of injustice as a causal factor in the
process leading to delinquent behavior.

> When a person ascribes his failure to injustice in the
> social system, he may criticize that system, bend his ef-
> forts toward reforming it, or disassociate himself from
> it—in other words, he may become alienated from the
> established set of social norms. He may even be con-
> vinced that he is justified in evading these norms in his
> pursuit of success-goals. . . .
> It is our impression that a sense of being unjustly de-
> prived of access to opportunities to which one is entitled
> is common among those who become participants in de-
> linquent subcultures (Cloward and Ohlin, 1960:111-12, 117).

Let us assume they are correct, that a "sense of being unjustly
deprived" is a causal factor in the development of delinquent subcultures
and of delinquent behavior. This implies that whatever contributes to
developing the sense of injustice is also an important causal factor in
the process. But one's view of what causes the sense of injustice will
differ according to whether one believes it to be accurate. In other
words, we will seek one set of causes for a sense of injustice when we
feel it is a response to objective injustice, and another set when we
feel it is not. If the sense of injustice is accurate, then the key causal
factors will lie in the objective injustice itself and those who perpetuate
it. If the sense of injustice is inaccurate, then we will seek causal
factors in those things that cause the individual to misperceive his situation. That is, if we agree that a "sense of injustice" is a proximate
cause of delinquency, and believe that it is an accurate perception of
objective injustice, then we will seek the more distant causes of delinquency in our unjust social institutions. If, however, we believe that
the sense of injustice is an illusion, then we shall seek the more distant
causes of delinquency in those factors (personal and otherwise) that
lead the delinquent to develop and sustain misperceptions and the un-
justness of his situation. Crudely speaking, in the first case we will
attribute the delinquency to institutional causes, and in the latter to individual and social psychological factors. All of this obviously depends
on our possessing a viable standard of justice against which to compare
the delinquent's "sense of injustice."

I wish to conclude with some general remarks about the broader
implications of Rawls's work for the study of criminology. Criminology
is the study of crime, which can be viewed either as "a violation of
criminal law" or as "a harm against society." There is, of course,

no reason to assume that these two areas will overlap everywhere. But if I might speculate, I would argue that the study of violations (or violators) of the criminal law is not the natural object of criminology as a social science. My reason for this perhaps paradoxical claim is that this would make criminology into a social science in which the object of study could be partially or totally changed by a legislator's act at any time. I doubt if there is any social science—surely no natural science—whose object of study could be changed or eliminated by legislative command. If we assume that a science should have as its object of study some coherent and relatively persistent group of phenomena, then criminology is significantly weakened by the fact that the very existence and shape of its object may be artificially maintained or arbitrarily altered. On the other hand, the notion of studying actions that are "harms to society" holds out the possibility of a coherent and relatively permanent object of study. My hunch is that criminologists have tended toward the legal definition of their field because of skepticism about objectively determining what is a harm to society. By simply accepting the legal definition of harm to society, however, the criminologist opens up the possibility of limiting his study to the boundaries of the ideology represented in the law, and placing his conclusions in the service of those who are served by that ideology. In short, the danger of ethical skepticism and ethical neutrality is that they may make a science the servant of institutions that are ethically quite partisan.

The point I wish to make is that the work being done on the concept of justice, especially the work of John Rawls, presents an alternative.[1] It offers an objective standard by which to determine what is and what is not a harm to society. It offers a standard that is not dependent on laws and thus is not subservient to lawmakers. It holds out to criminology the independence that should mark truly scientific inquiry.

Notes

1. In this general area of philosophy, the work of Kurt Baier is also of considerable importance. Readers of Baier's The Moral Point of View: A Rational Basis of Ethics (New York: Random House, 1965) will no doubt recognize the degree to which the present discussion is indebted to his treatment of fundamental moral notions.

References

Cloward, R. A., and L. Ohlin
    1960   Delinquency and Opportunity. New York: Free Press.
Matza, D.
    1964   Delinquency and Drift. New York: John Wiley.
Quinney, R.
    1970   The Social Reality of Crime. Boston: Little, Brown.
Rawls, J.
    1971   A Theory of Justice. Cambridge, Mass.: Harvard Univer-
            sity Press.

Editors

Marc Riedel, Ph.D., University of Pennsylvania, 1972. Director, Death Penalty and Discretion Project, Center for Studies in Criminology and Criminal Law, University of Pennsylvania; Assistant Professor, School of Social Work, University of Pennsylvania; Criminology Book Review Editor, Journal of Criminal Law and Criminology; Assistant Editor, Criminology: An Interdisciplinary Journal; coeditor of Treating the Offender; Issues in Criminal Justice; Police: Problems and Prospects; American Society; Sociological Perspectives.

Duncan Chappell, Ph.D., University of Cambridge, 1965. Director, Law and Justice Study Center, Battelle Memorial Institute, Human Affairs Research Center; Adjunct Associate Professor of Sociology, University of Washington; Consultant, U.S. Senate Select Committee on Small Business, Criminal Redistribution Systems; coauthor, The Police and the Public in Australia and New Zealand; coeditor, The Australian Criminal Justice System, Violence and Criminal Justice.

Contributors

Stuart Adams, Ph.D., Ohio State University, 1948. Visiting Research Fellow, National Institute of Law Enforcement and Criminal Justice, Washington, D.C.

Richard A. Ball, Ph.D., Ohio State University, 1965. Associate Professor of Sociology, West Virginia University.

Hugo Adam Bedau, Ph.D., Harvard University, 1961. Austin B. Fletcher Professor of Philosophy, Tufts University.

Richard Block, Ph.D., University of Chicago, 1969. Associate Professor of Sociology, Loyola University of Chicago.

James Boudouris, Ph.D., Wayne State University, 1970. Assistant Professor of Sociology, College of Saint Teresa.

Brian L. Hollander, LL.B., New York University Law School, 1965. President, Hartford Institute of Criminal and Social Justice, Inc.

Barry Krisberg, Ph.D., University of Pennsylvania, 1971. Assistant Professor of Criminology, University of California, Berkeley.

Joseph S. Lobenthal, Jr., J.D., University of Chicago, 1955. Attorney and legal consultant, New York City; Adjunct Professor, New York University Law School.

Leonard M. Lieberman, M.A., Sangamon State University, 1971. State Government Liaison, Illinois Law Enforcement Commission.

Milton Luger, M.A., New York University, 1950. Director, New York State Division for Youth.

Jeffrey H. Reiman, Ph.D., Pennsylvania State University, 1968. Associate Professor, Center for the Administration of Justice, American University.

David J. Ross, M.A., Loyola University of Chicago, 1975. Research Associate, Department of Sociology, Loyola University of Chicago.

Leonard Rutman, Ph.D., University of Minnesota. Assistant Professor, School of Social Work, Carleton University.

Paul Takagi, Ph.D., Stanford University, 1966. Associate Professor, School of Criminology, University of California, Berkeley.

CORRECTIONS: PROBLEMS OF PUNISHMENT AND REHABILITATION
edited by Edward Sagarin
and Donal E. J. MacNamara

CRIME AND DELINQUENCY: DIMENSIONS OF DEVIANCE
edited by Marc Riedel
and Terence P. Thornberry

CRIME PREVENTION AND SOCIAL CONTROL
edited by Ronald L. Akers
and Edward Sagarin

IMAGES OF CRIME: OFFENDERS AND VICTIMS
edited by Terence P. Thornberry
and Edward Sagarin